Chocolat

ERIC LANLARD

Photography by Kate Whitaker

Chocolat

SEDUCTIVE RECIPES FOR BAKES, DESSERTS, TRUFFLES AND OTHER TREATS

ERIC LANLARD

Photography by Kate Whitaker

MITCHELL BEAZLEY

To Paul and Bobby, for their continuous support.

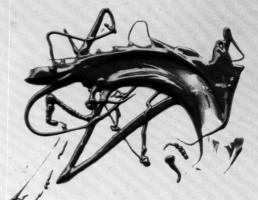

First published in Great Britain in 2013 by Mitchell Beazley,
an imprint of Octopus Publishing Group Ltd,
Endeavour House, 189 Shaftesbury Avenue,
London WC2H 8JY
www.octopusbooks.co.uk

An Hachette UK Company
www.hachette.co.uk

British Library Cataloguing-in-Publication Data.
A catalogue record for this book is available from the
British Library.

Publisher Alison Starling
Art direction and design Juliette Norsworthy
Senior editor Sybella Stephens
Home economists Rachel Wood, Wendy Lee
Photography Kate Whitaker
Prop stylist Liz Belton
Production Caroline Alberti

ISBN: 978 1 84533 694 3
Printed and bound in China

All recipes have been tested in metric.
Medium eggs and whole milk should be used,
unless otherwise stated.

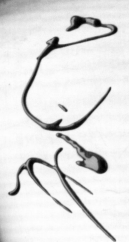

Contents

Introduction

At the age of ten, my attraction to chocolate – the 'food of the gods' – had already started. In fact, my memories go much further back to my family's daily visits to the local boulangerie, where we would buy a brioche and a single bar of dark 'Chocolat Poulain' – the trick was to push the bar up without breaking it and enjoy it on the way to school. The reason that, years later, I chose Le Grand Pâtisserie in Quimper for my apprenticeship is because it was the only local boutique that made its own chocolate!

My fascination with this precious ingredient is still with me and over the years I have made it my mission to discover the history and origins of chocolate, and the techniques of its production. To understand the whole process, from cocoa bean to an indulgent, finished product, I have been lucky enough to walk through a fertile hacienda in South America and a plantation in Trinidad, to touch, taste and smell the raw ingredient and then witness the long process of the cocoa beans being roasted, conched, blended and moulded into delicious chocolate bars, eggs or other fabulous shapes.

But as much as I adore eating chocolate, it's as a baking ingredient that I love it the most and with this new book I want to share my passion for chocolate with you. From indulgent chocolate drinks, tarts, muffins and mousses to gâteaux, petits fours and elaborate creations for special occasions, join me in the madness of baking with chocolate!

Eric ✗

A brief history of chocolate

Originating in the rainforests of Central America, the cacao tree was first cultivated as early as 1500BC by the Olmecs, followed later by the Maya and the Aztec peoples, who enjoyed a beverage called *chocolati* (bitter water). The drink was made by roasting and crushing cocoa beans on hot stone, then the rich paste was mixed into hot water with the addition of vanilla, pepper, cinnamon and aniseed. It was enjoyed as a nourishing, power-busting drink and aphrodisiac. The Maya and the Aztec peoples also used the precious beans as money – taxes and slave transactions were paid and made with cocoa beans.

In 1519, the conquistador Hernán Cortés reached modern-day Mexico and began the conquest of that country. The Aztec emperor Montezuma gave Cortés a cup of freshly prepared cocoa, who later wrote: 'After drinking this elixir you could just go on and on and travel the world without fatigues and without need for other food.' In 1524, Cortés sent Charles I of Spain a cargo of cocoa beans and the king of Spain and his court enjoyed the delights of this precious ingredient, adding honey to it to make it sweeter. Spain kept its monopoly of the cocoa trade for years until it started to appear all over Europe during the 17th century, especially in Italy, France and Great Britain.

As chocolate grew more popular, the way to treat it became more sophisticated, with new techniques and machinery introduced, but it wasn't until 1802 that the Italians fully industrialized chocolate production. Milk chocolate was first made by a Swiss named Daniel Peter in 1875, and his compatriot Rodolphe Lindt invented the conching process to refine the texture of chocolate, which revolutionized the way chocolate is made and eaten.

The production process

My favourite treat begins its life inside a cocoa pod, which grow on trees in the tropics of West Africa, Southeast Asia and South America (the best varieties are grown on small family farms or haciendas) – the cocoa beans, from which chocolate is made, are the seeds of the cacao tree found within the pod.

The cocoa pods are harvested and taken to cooperatives where they are opened. The seeds and pulp are scooped out, then fermented and dried. The cocoa beans are then taken abroad to be processed. The dried beans, like coffee, are roasted and crushed, then the husks are removed and the cocoa nibs are pressed through rollers to make 'chocolate liquor'. After more pressing, the combination of cooling and heating processes and the addition of sugar and other ingredients, the final precious product runs free from the heavy machinery and is then transformed into bars, buttons and chips ready to be eaten or used in baking.

Know your chocolate

How to choose a good chocolate

Choosing a good chocolate is first a question of taste. In its raw state, cacao is bitter, so the taste and quality of chocolate depends on the percentage of cocoa solids it contains, the provenance of the cocoa beans and the production process. A good-quality chocolate has a shiny finish and is brittle, with a strong characteristic taste and smoothness, and it should not stick to the palate. A premium chocolate will also have mostly cocoa butter as its main fat content. For baking or making desserts, I personally like to use chocolate with a maximum of 70% cocoa solids, as chocolate with a higher percentage of cocoa solids can be too bitter.

Storing chocolate

Avoid storing chocolate in the refrigerator – keep it in a cool (15–20°C/59–68°F), dry and dark place away from strong odours like spices, strong foods or other cooking smells.

If your chocolate has a white discoloration on its surface (chocolate bloom), it is best to discard it, as that means it is old or has been stored in extreme temperatures.

Working with chocolate

Melting chocolate

In a bain-marie

The classic way to melt chocolate is in a heatproof bowl set over a saucepan of barely simmering water. For a great result, the secret is to melt the chocolate gently over a very low heat, making sure the surface of the water does not touch the bowl.

In a microwave

Alternatively, you can put chocolate into a microwavable bowl and zap it in the microwave on high power for few seconds at a time, stirring gently in between bursts, until melted. Every microwave is different, so it is worth testing a small amount of chocolate in your microwave first, to see how long it takes to melt. Remember, milk and white chocolate burn more easily than dark chocolate, so be very cautious and gentle when melting them, whichever process you use.

Tempering chocolate

What is tempering?

Tempering is a technique that pastry chefs and chocolatiers use to stabilize chocolate and achieve a glossy, hard, brittle finish, making tempered chocolate perfect for dipping individual chocolates and truffles or coating biscuits and cakes. It involves melting and cooling chocolate, then bringing it to the correct temperature for coating.

The technique

For best results, use a chocolate or sugar thermometer to check that the correct temperature for each stage has been reached.

First, if using a bar of chocolate, chop your chocolate as finely as possible. Melt two-thirds of it in a heatproof bowl set over a saucepan of barely simmering water (see Melting chocolate on page 11). Remove the bowl from the pan when the chocolate is just melted and has reached the required temperature (see chart opposite). Add the remaining chocolate a little at the time, stirring gently between additions. Continue to stir gently until all the chocolate is melted and the mixture has cooled to 26–27°C (79–81°F) (see chart opposite).

Return the bowl of melted chocolate to the pan and reheat to 28–30°C (82–86°F) (see chart opposite). To test, drizzle a few drops of the chocolate on to a piece of baking paper – the chocolate should set in a few minutes and be ready for use. If it sets too fast, return the bowl to the pan and heat for a few seconds to make it more fluid. Use for dipping and coating.

Chocolate Tempering Temperatures

Chocolate	Melted Temperature	Cooled Temperature	Reheated Temperature
Dark	50°C (122°F)	27°C (81°F)	30°C (86°F)
Milk	45°C (113°F)	27°C (81°F)	29°C (84°F)
White	40°C (104°F)	26°C (79°F)	28°C (82°F)

Chocolate and vanilla marble cake

From the Bakery

Chocolate and vanilla marble cake

This recipe is one of my earliest baking recipes. I used to make it every Wednesday when I was off school – it's fun and easy to make, and a great teatime treat.

Serves 8

Preparation time: 15 minutes, plus cooling

Cooking time: 50 minutes

125g (4oz) unsalted butter, melted and cooled, plus extra for greasing

125g (4oz) dark chocolate, roughly chopped

5 eggs, separated

125g (4oz) golden caster sugar

125g (4oz) plain flour

2 tsp baking powder

2 tsp vanilla extract or paste

Preheat the oven to 180°C (fan 160°C)/350°F/gas mark 4. Grease a 900g (2lb) loaf tin and line with baking paper.

Melt the chocolate in a heatproof bowl set over a saucepan of barely simmering water, making sure the surface of the water does not touch the bowl.

In a large bowl, whisk the egg yolks and sugar together using an electric hand whisk until pale. Beat in the cooled, melted butter, then sift in the flour and baking powder and fold in.

Separate the mixture into 2 large bowls. Fold the vanilla into one of the mixtures and the melted chocolate into the other. In a large, clean, dry bowl, whisk the egg whites to stiff peaks, then gently fold half of the egg whites into each cake mixture.

Spoon layers of the mixtures alternately into the prepared tin, then run through a skewer 2–3 times to create a marbled effect. Bake in the oven for 45 minutes, or until a skewer inserted into the centre comes out clean. Leave to cool in the tin for 10 minutes, then turn out on to a cooling rack to cool completely. See previous page for the finished result.

Tip

To make the cake even more luxurious, coat it with melted dark chocolate.

1. Whisk the egg yolks and sugar together until pale.

2. Beat in the melted butter, then fold in the flour and baking powder.

3. Divide between 2 bowls and add the melted chocolate to one bowl.

4. Make sure both the vanilla and chocolate are thoroughly mixed in.

5. Divide the whisked egg whites between the 2 mixtures and gently fold in.

6. Alternately spoon the dark and light mixtures into the tin and run a skewer through the mix to create the marbled effect.

Chocolate and cinnamon buns

When I travel to the USA I always make a point of going to the local bakery or food hall to get some freshly baked cinnamon buns. The aroma is so spicy, sweet and moreish. I like them dripping with icing, and these, of course, include my other favourite ingredient – chocolate!

Makes 11

Preparation time: 30 minutes, plus rising

Cooking time: 25–30 minutes

500ml (17fl oz) warm milk

150g (5oz) golden caster sugar

40g (1½oz) fresh yeast or 2 x (7g) sachets easy-bake dried yeast

200g (7oz) unsalted butter, melted, plus extra for greasing

2 tsp vanilla paste or extract

1 egg, plus 1 egg, beaten

1kg (2lb) plain flour, plus extra for dusting

For the filling

75g (3oz) dark chocolate, grated

100g (3½oz) unsalted butter, melted and cooled

200g (7oz) dark muscovado sugar

3 tbsp ground cinnamon

For the glaze

75g (3oz) golden icing sugar

1 tsp vanilla extract

1 tbsp water

Start by making the dough. Put the milk, sugar, yeast, melted butter, vanilla and whole egg into the bowl of a freestanding mixer fitted with a dough hook, then mix together until smooth. Sift the flour, then gradually add to the bowl, mixing until the dough comes away from the side of the bowl. Place the dough in a large, lightly floured bowl and cover with clingfilm or a damp tea towel. Leave to rise for 45 minutes–1 hour at room temperature, or until the dough has almost doubled in volume.

To make the filling, beat the grated chocolate, cooled melted butter, sugar and cinnamon in a bowl to a smooth, spreadable paste and put to one side.

When the dough has risen, knock it back to release the air, then turn out on to a lightly floured surface. Roll out the dough to an 8mm (½in) thick rectangle, about 28 x 70cm (11 x 27in). Using a palette knife, spread the filling all over the dough. Starting at a long edge, roll the dough into a long sausage shape without stretching it. Using a sharp knife, cut into slices about 6cm (2½in) wide. Place them on 2 greased and floured baking sheets. Cover with clingfilm or a damp tea towel and leave to rise for 30 minutes.

Preheat the oven to 200°C (fan 180°C)/400°F/gas mark 6. Meanwhile, add the water to the beaten egg to make an egg wash. Use a pastry brush and lightly brush the tops of the buns with the egg wash.

Bake the buns in the oven for 10 minutes, then reduce the heat to 180°C (fan 160°C)/350°F/gas mark 4 and cook for a further 15–20 minutes, or until golden brown, cooked in the centre and the buns sound hollow when tapped on the bases.

Meanwhile, to make the glaze, mix the icing sugar, vanilla and water together in a bowl. As soon as the buns are cooked, brush them generously with the glaze and leave to cool. These are fantastic served with coffee or hot chocolate.

Pain au chocolat

After the croissant, the pain au chocolat is probably the most popular breakfast food in France. I certainly grew up eating these lovely flaky pastries on my way to school. This recipe requires you to wake up a bit early to make them, but it's worth it, especially for a weekend treat.

Makes 6

Preparation time: 40 minutes, plus rising and chilling

Cooking time: 25–30 minutes

250ml (8fl oz) warm milk

1 tsp dried yeast

165g (5½oz) unsalted butter, plus extra for greasing

40g (1½oz) golden caster sugar

1 tsp salt

450g (14½oz) plain flour, sifted, plus extra for dusting

200g (7oz) dark chocolate bar, broken into 12 strips

1 egg, beaten

Put the milk, yeast, 15g (½oz) of the butter, the sugar and salt into the bowl of a freestanding mixer fitted with a dough hook, then mix well. Gradually add the flour, mixing until the dough comes away from the side of the bowl. Place the dough in a lightly floured bowl and cover with clingfilm or a damp tea towel. Leave to rise for 40 minutes at room temperature, or until the dough has almost doubled in volume.

Using a rolling pin, lightly beat the remaining butter between 2 sheets of greaseproof paper to a rectangle, 12 x 20cm (5 x 8in), and chill.

When the dough has risen, knock it back to release the air, then turn out on to a floured surface. Roll out the dough to a rectangle, 20 x 40cm (8 x 16in). Remove the butter from the greaseproof paper and place in the centre of the dough. Fold the dough over the butter like an envelope, making sure none of the butter is exposed.

Roll out the dough to an even rectangle, 20 x 50cm (8 x 20in). Fold the dough in thirds lengthways, like a business letter. This completes the first turn. Rotate by 90 degrees so that the folded edge is on your left and the dough faces you like a book. Roll out again to a neat rectangle, 20 x 50cm (8 x 20in), and repeat the folding process. This completes the second turn. Cover with clingfilm and chill in the refrigerator for at least 30 minutes. Repeat the process so that you end up with 4 turns in total, then chill for a further 30 minutes.

Roll out the dough on a floured surface to a 5mm (¼in) thick rectangle, 20 x 60cm (8 x 24in), then cut into 6 strips, about 10 x 20cm (4 x 8in). Place 2 strips of chocolate across the shorter length of a dough strip and roll up, enclosing the chocolate. Repeat with the remaining chocolate and dough strips. Place seam side down on a greased baking sheet and flatten them gently with your hand. Cover with clingfilm and leave to rise at room temperature for 35–40 minutes.

Preheat the oven to 180°C (fan 160°C)/350°F/gas mark 4. Brush the pastries with the beaten egg and bake in the oven for 25–30 minutes, or until golden brown. Leave to cool before serving.

Devilish chocolate brownies

I know there are plenty of brownie recipes around, but this is my favourite dark chocolate version, and, of course, you can add nuts or dried fruits if you like. Remember, don't overcook them.

Makes 16

Preparation time: 10 minutes

Cooking time: 30 minutes

200g (7oz) dark chocolate, roughly chopped

150g (5oz) unsalted butter, plus extra for greasing

2 tsp vanilla paste or extract

150g (5oz) golden caster sugar

3 eggs, beaten

75g (3oz) plain flour

2 tbsp cocoa powder

1 tsp salt

100g (3½oz) dark chocolate chips

Preheat the oven to 180°C (fan 160°C)/350°F/gas mark 4. Grease a 19cm (7½in) square shallow baking tin and line the base with baking paper.

Melt the chopped chocolate, butter and vanilla together in a heatproof bowl set over a saucepan of barely simmering water, making sure the surface of the water does not touch the bowl. Remove from the heat and stir in the sugar, then leave to cool for a few minutes.

Beat in the eggs, then sift in the flour, cocoa and salt and fold in until the mixture is smooth and glossy. Stir in the chocolate chips.

Pour the mixture into the prepared tin and level the top. Bake in the oven for 25 minutes, or until the top starts to crack but the centre remains gooey. Turn off the oven and leave the brownies inside for a further 5 minutes before removing. Leave to cool completely in the tin.

Cut the brownies into 16 small squares and remove from the tin. Store in an airtight container for up to 4 days.

Chocolate Kouign Amann

Kouign Amann is a speciality from my native Brittany – it was invented by a pâtissier in the city of Douarnenez. The translation of the Breton name is 'butter cake' and you will understand why when making it. This is my chocolate version.

Serves 12

Preparation time: 45 minutes, plus chilling and rising

Cooking time: 25–30 minutes

75g (3oz) unsalted butter, plus extra for greasing

8g (¼oz) fresh yeast or 1 tsp dried yeast

80ml (3fl oz) warm water

200g (7oz) plain flour, plus extra for dusting

1 tsp salt

125g (4oz) slightly salted butter

150g (5oz) golden caster sugar

50g (2oz) dark chocolate, grated

Melt 50g (2oz) of the unsalted butter in a small saucepan. Put the yeast into a bowl and dissolve in the water, then mix in the melted butter.

Sift the flour and salt together into a large bowl. Make a well in the centre, add the yeast mixture and gradually mix together to form a dough. Turn out on to a floured surface and knead the dough for 10 minutes until smooth and elastic. Cover with clingfilm and chill in the refrigerator for at least 30 minutes.

Using a rolling pin, lightly beat the slightly salted butter between 2 sheets of greaseproof paper to form a rectangle, 12 x 20cm (5 x 8in). Place in the refrigerator with the dough.

Roll out the dough on a lightly floured surface to a 30cm (12in) disc. Place the chilled butter in the centre, then sprinkle over one-quarter of the sugar and grated chocolate. Fold the dough over the butter like an envelope, making sure none of the butter is exposed. Beat the dough slightly with the rolling pin, then roll out to an even rectangle, 20 x 40cm (8 x 16in).

Using a pastry brush, remove any flour from the dough. Fold the dough in thirds lengthways, like a business letter. This completes the first turn. Rotate by 90 degrees so that the folded edge is on your left and the dough faces you like a book. Roll out again to a neat rectangle, 20 x 40cm (8 x 16in). Sprinkle over another quarter of the sugar and chocolate and repeat the folding process. This completes the second turn. Cover with clingfilm and chill in the refrigerator for 30 minutes. Repeat the process, then cover and chill for a further 30 minutes.

Preheat the oven to 200°C (fan 180°C)/400°F/gas mark 6. Grease and flour a 30cm (12in) square baking tin.

Roll out the dough on a floured surface to a 30cm (12in) square. Fold each corner into the middle and turn upside down into the tin. Melt the remaining unsalted butter in a saucepan, then brush liberally over the top. Sprinkle with the remaining sugar and chocolate. Leave to rise at room temperature for 25 minutes.

Bake in the oven for 25–30 minutes, or until golden and caramelized. Remove from the tin before completely cool, as the caramel will stick. This is best eaten hot with a traditional little glass of local Calvados!

White chocolate and lemon madeleines

Madeleines have had a huge revival recently, mostly as petits fours in restaurants. I prefer them full-size, as they don't dry out so quickly, and these chocolate versions will keep very well in an airtight tin or cookie jar.

Makes 36
Preparation time: 15 minutes
Cooking time: 35 minutes

300g (10oz) plain flour, plus extra for dusting
125g (4oz) white chocolate, roughly chopped
4 eggs
225g (7½oz) golden caster sugar
125g (4oz) unsalted butter, plus extra for greasing
1½ tsp baking powder
grated zest of 1 lemon

Preheat the oven to 180°C (fan 160°C)/350°F/gas mark 4. Grease and lightly flour a 12-hole madeleine tin.

Melt the butter and chocolate together in a heatproof bowl set over a saucepan of barely simmering water, making sure the surface of the water does not touch the bowl. Leave to cool for a few minutes.

In a large bowl, whisk the eggs and sugar together using an electric hand whisk for several minutes until pale and foamy, then whisk in the cooled butter and chocolate mixture. Sift the flour and baking powder together, then gently fold into the mixture. Beat in the lemon zest until the mixture is smooth and glossy.

Spoon the mixture into the holes of the prepared tin, filling them three-quarters full. Bake in the oven for 10 minutes, or until a light golden colour. Transfer immediately to a cooling rack. Repeat with the remaining mixture.

Tip

Use a low heat to melt white chocolate, as it can burn very easily.

Mini red velvet cakes with white chocolate frosting

This all-American favourite is now a worldwide sensation, and the use of oil and buttermilk make it extremely moist. My twist on the frosting makes this version even more indulgent.

Makes 6

Preparation time: 40 minutes, plus cooling

Cooking time: 40 minutes

butter, for greasing
225g (7½oz) golden caster sugar
2 eggs
275 ml (9fl oz) vegetable oil
125ml (4fl oz) buttermilk
1 tbsp red food colouring
1 tsp vanilla extract
175g (6oz) plain flour
15g (½oz) cocoa powder
½ tsp baking powder
½ tsp salt
2 tsp white wine vinegar
icing sugar, for dusting

For the frosting
75g (3oz) white chocolate, roughly chopped
175g (6oz) unsalted butter, softened
375g (12oz) icing sugar
2 tbsp milk

Preheat the oven to 180°C (fan 160°C)/350°F/gas mark 4. Grease 7 x 6cm (2½in) diameter cooking rings 4cm (1½in) deep, line with baking paper, and place on a baking sheet lined with baking paper.

In a large bowl, whisk the eggs and sugar together using an electric hand whisk until pale. On slow speed, add the oil a little at a time until it has all been incorporated. Beat in the buttermilk, food colouring and vanilla. Sift the flour, cocoa powder, baking powder and salt together, then fold in, followed by the vinegar.

Divide the mixture between the cake rings, filling them three-quarters full. Bake in the oven for 35 minutes, or until a skewer inserted into the centres comes out clean.

Leave to cool in the rings for 5 minutes, then remove the cakes from the rings to a cooling rack to cool completely.

To make the frosting, melt the chocolate in a heatproof bowl set over a saucepan of barely simmering water, making sure the surface of the water does not touch the bowl. Leave to cool. Beat the butter and half the icing sugar together until smooth, then add the remaining icing sugar a little at a time, beating until the mixture is smooth. Add the milk and cooled chocolate and beat for a further 2 minutes.

To assemble, slice a mini cake horizontally into 3 layers. Thinly spread a layer of frosting on to the base layer, then sandwich the middle layer on top. Spread a little more frosting on the middle layer, then add the top layer. Repeat with 5 of the mini cakes so that you have 6 cakes in total leaving one spare. Spoon the remaining frosting into a piping bag fitted with a plain piping nozzle, then pipe around the edges of the cakes until completely covered. Crumble the remaining mini cake and sprinkle the crumbs over the tops of the piped cakes. Serve dusted with icing sugar.

Flour-free chocolate sponge

This is a great recipe, as the lack of flour makes this sponge really soft and moist and it is gluten free, too. It's so dark and chocolaty that I usually serve it with a little whipped cream and some fresh berries.

Serves 6
Preparation time: 10 minutes
Cooking time: 40 minutes

125g (4oz) dark chocolate, roughly chopped

125g (4oz) unsalted butter, softened, plus extra for greasing

150g (5oz) golden caster sugar

3 eggs, beaten

1 tsp vanilla paste or extract

75g (3oz) cocoa powder

Preheat the oven to 170°C (fan 150°C)/325°F/gas mark 3. Grease a 20cm (8in) diameter, 6cm (2½ in) deep springform cake tin and line with baking paper.

Melt the chocolate in a heatproof bowl set over a saucepan of barely simmering water, making sure the surface of the water does not touch the bowl. Leave to cool.

In a large bowl, cream the butter and sugar together using an electric hand whisk until pale and fluffy. Beat in the eggs one at a time, followed by the cooled chocolate and the vanilla. Sift the cocoa powder and gently fold in.

Spoon the mixture into the prepared tin and bake in the oven for 35 minutes, or until a skewer inserted into the centre comes out clean. Leave to cool in the tin for 10 minutes, then turn out on to a cooling rack.

Tip

For an extra hit of cocoa, dust the inside of the greased tin with cocoa powder.

Soft cookie dough cookies

I simply adore these cookies. I love the soft centres, the rich flavour of the unrefined sugar and all the additions of nuts, chocolate chips or dried fruits, which make them so moreish and delicious.

Makes 24

Preparation time: 15 minutes

Cooking time: 25–30 minutes

175g (6oz) unsalted butter, melted

200g (7oz) dark muscovado sugar

100g (3½oz) golden caster sugar

1 tsp vanilla extract or paste

2 eggs

250g (8oz) plain flour

½ tsp bicarbonate of soda

½ tsp salt

100g (3½oz) dark chocolate chips

100g (3½oz) white chocolate chips

100g (3½oz) macadamia nuts, roughly chopped

Preheat the oven to 180°C (fan 160°C)/350°F/gas mark 4. Line 2 baking sheets with baking paper.

In a large bowl, cream the melted butter, muscovado sugar and caster sugar together until smooth. Beat in the vanilla and eggs until light and creamy.

Sift the flour, bicarbonate of soda and salt together, then fold into the butter and sugar mixture until just combined. Stir in the chocolate chips and nuts.

Using an ice-cream scoop if possible, scoop the dough on to the prepared baking sheets, leaving at least 8cm (3½in) between each cookie, as they will spread in the oven. Do not flatten them before baking.

Bake in the oven for 12–15 minutes, or until the edges look golden brown but the centre is still soft. Leave to cool on the baking sheets for 5 minutes, then carefully transfer to a cooling rack to cool completely. Repeat with any remaining dough. Store the cookies in an airtight tin for up to a few days.

Tip

To vary the flavour, substitute the chocolate chips and macadamia nuts with dried fruits and different nuts.

Dark chocolate moelleux

This extremely moist sponge is a perfect base for a celebration cake filled with a rich chocolate buttercream and coated with a glossy ganache. It looks great decorated with berries or dried fruits and nuts.

Serves 12–14

Preparation time: 30 minutes, plus cooling and setting

Cooking time: 40–45 minutes

50g (2oz) dark chocolate, roughly chopped

350g (11½oz) butter, softened, plus extra for greasing

350g (11½oz) golden caster sugar

50g (2oz) black treacle

8 eggs, lightly beaten

300g (10oz) self-raising flour

50g (2oz) cocoa powder

2 tsp baking powder

50g (2oz) ground almonds

berries or dried fruits and nuts, to decorate

icing sugar, for dusting

For the ganache
200ml (7fl oz) whipping cream

200g (7oz) dark chocolate, chopped

For the buttercream
25g (1oz) dark chocolate, roughly chopped

200g (7oz) icing sugar, sifted

100g (3½ oz) unsalted butter, softened

a few drops of vanilla extract

2 tbsp double cream

First make the sponge. Preheat the oven to 170°C (fan 150°C)/325°F/gas mark 3. Grease 2 x 22cm (8½in) diameter sandwich cake tins and line with baking paper. Melt the chocolate in a heatproof bowl set over a saucepan of barely simmering water, making sure the surface of the water does not touch the bowl.

In a large bowl, cream the butter and sugar together until light and fluffy, then beat in the black treacle. Beat in the eggs a little at a time, then add the melted chocolate. Sift the flour, cocoa powder and baking powder together, then fold in with the ground almonds. Finish with an electric hand whisk to produce a smooth, glossy consistency.

Divide the mixture between the prepared tins and level the tops. Bake in the oven for 30–35 minutes, or until a skewer inserted into the centres comes out clean. Leave to cool in the tins, then turn out on to a cooling rack.

To make the ganache, put the whipping cream into a saucepan and heat to just below boiling point. Remove from the heat and add the chocolate, then use a wooden spoon to beat vigorously until melted and smooth. Leave to cool to room temperature.

To make the buttercream, melt the chocolate as above and leave to cool. In a bowl, cream the icing sugar and butter together using an electric hand whisk until light and fluffy. Beat in the vanilla, cooled chocolate and double cream to form a fairly stiff spreading consistency.

To assemble the cake, level the tops of the sponges using a sharp knife. Spread the buttercream over the top of one of the sponges and place it on a cooling rack set over a large plate or baking tray. Place the other sponge, upside down, on top to give a nice flat surface. Pour the ganache over the cake, completely covering it. Smooth with a palette knife and leave to set at room temperature. Serve decorated with berries or dried fruits and nuts, and lightly dusted with icing sugar.

Chocolate gâteau Basque

This is a speciality from southwest France, just on the Spanish border. I've given this traditional gâteau a chocolate twist, which works wonders.

Serves 8–10

Preparation time: 30 minutes, plus chilling

Cooking time: 40–45 minutes

250g (8oz) unsalted butter, softened, plus extra for greasing

200g (7oz) light muscovado sugar

125g (4oz) ground almonds

1 large egg

1 tsp vanilla paste or extract

300g (10oz) plain flour, plus extra for dusting

1 tsp baking powder

15g (½oz) cocoa powder

1 egg yolk, beaten

For the chocolate custard

500ml (17fl oz) milk

125ml (4fl oz) single cream

50g (2oz) semolina

1 vanilla pod, split lengthways

150g (5oz) dark chocolate, finely chopped

2 egg yolks

150g (5oz) golden caster sugar

25g (1oz) plain flour

In a large bowl, beat together the butter, muscovado sugar, ground almonds, egg and vanilla. Sift in the flour, baking powder and cocoa powder, then combine together to form a dough without over-kneading. Cover with clingfilm and leave to rest in the refrigerator for at least 1 hour.

Meanwhile, make the custard. Put the milk, cream, semolina and vanilla pod into a saucepan and bring to the boil. Remove the vanilla pod. Add the chocolate and stir until melted, then remove from the heat. Mix the 2 egg yolks with the caster sugar in a bowl, then add the flour and beat until smooth. Pour a little of the hot chocolate milk on to the yolk mixture. Whisk well and pour back into the saucepan. Bring back to the boil and simmer for 2 minutes, whisking continuously. Transfer to a bowl and cover with clingfilm. Leave to cool.

Preheat the oven to 180°C (fan 160°C)/350°F/gas mark 4. Grease and flour a 22cm (8½in) diameter, 5cm (2in) deep round cake tin.

Roll out two-thirds of the pastry on a floured surface and carefully use to line the tin. If the pastry splits, gently mould it back together. Fill with the cold custard.

Roll out the remaining pastry to a disc large enough to cover the top of the tin.

Brush the edge of the pastry inside the tin with the beaten egg. Cover with the pastry disc, then trim the edge and seal. Brush the top with more beaten egg and lightly mark the top in a criss-cross design using a fork.

Place the tin on a wire rack over a baking tray, then bake in the oven for 35–40 minutes, or until golden. Leave to cool completely before removing from the tin and serving.

Chocolate and hazelnut muffins

Most muffin recipes come as a fruity option for breakfast. These rich muffins are more a mid-afternoon treat when served warm straight from the oven.

Makes 6

Preparation time: 15 minutes

Cooking time: 25–30 minutes

75g (3oz) dark chocolate, roughly chopped

50g (2oz) chocolate and hazelnut spread

175g (6oz) self-raising flour

½ tbsp baking powder

25g (1oz) cocoa powder

50g (2oz) golden caster sugar

2 eggs

1 tsp vanilla extract or paste

5 tbsp vegetable oil

4 tbsp milk

75g (3oz) dark chocolate chips

50g (2oz) chopped hazelnuts, roasted (see Tip on page 44)

Preheat the oven to 180°C (fan 160°C)/350°F/gas mark 4. Line a 6-hole deep muffin tin with paper muffin cases.

Gently melt the chocolate and chocolate spread together in a heatproof bowl set over a saucepan of barely simmering water, making sure the surface of the water does not touch the bowl. Leave to cool for a few minutes.

Sift the flour, baking powder and cocoa powder into a large bowl, then stir in the sugar. In a separate bowl, beat the eggs, vanilla, oil and milk together using an electric hand whisk. When combined, stir in the cooled chocolate. Fold the wet ingredients into the dry ingredients using a rubber spatula or metal spoon, but don't over-mix. Stir in the chocolate chips.

Divide the mixture between the muffin cases, filling them three-quarters full, then sprinkle the hazelnuts over the tops. Bake in the oven for 20–25 minutes, or until a skewer inserted into the centres comes out clean. When cooked, transfer to a cooling rack to cool.

Tip

This recipe will make 12 small cakes if you use a shallow bun tin.

Chocolate pain d'épice

Pain d'épice is a speciality from the east of France; this sticky loaf is usually served toasted with a spread of butter. This is my take on the traditional recipe, making it even more indulgent with chocolate.

Serves 8
Preparation time: 15 minutes, plus overnight chilling
Cooking time: 50–55 minutes

butter, for greasing
200ml (7fl oz) milk
8 tbsp clear honey
125g (4oz) dark chocolate, finely chopped
300g (10oz) wholemeal flour
65g (2½oz) light muscovado sugar
1 tsp bicarbonate of soda
½ tsp ground cinnamon
½ tsp freshly grated nutmeg
½ tsp ground ginger
¼ tsp ground cloves
3 eggs, beaten
1 tbsp vanilla extract or paste
1 tbsp orange blossom water

Grease a 900g (2lb) loaf tin and line with baking paper.

Put the milk and honey into a small saucepan and heat gently but do not let it boil. Remove from the heat and add the chocolate, stirring until melted and blended together. Leave to cool for a few minutes.

Put the flour, sugar, bicarbonate of soda and spices into a large bowl and mix together. Make a well in the centre, then stir in the eggs, vanilla and orange blossom water, followed by the chocolate milk.

For best results, transfer the mixture to a food processor and blend for 2–3 minutes, or until smooth and very glossy. Alternatively, mix well using a wooden spoon. Pour the mixture into the prepared loaf tin, cover with clingfilm and leave to rest in the refrigerator overnight.

Bake the loaf in a preheated oven, 180°C (fan 160°C)/ 350°F/gas mark 4, for 45–50 minutes, or until a skewer inserted into the centre comes out clean. Leave to cool in the tin for 5 minutes, then transfer to a cooling rack to cool completely. The loaf keeps very well wrapped in clingfilm in an airtight container for up to 2 weeks.

Tip

Try toasting slices of this cake and spreading with butter or honey to serve.

Double chocolate macaroons

Macaroons are still very popular and fashionable, with more and more extraordinary flavours available. For me, you cannot beat a rich dark chocolate macaroon. I call these ones double as they are sandwiched together with chocolate filling, too.

Makes 28

Preparation time: 30 minutes, plus standing and cooling

Cooking time: 25 minutes

200g (7oz) icing sugar

125g (4oz) ground almonds

15g (½oz) cocoa powder

3 egg whites

25g (1oz) golden caster sugar

red paste food colouring

finely chopped dark chocolate, to decorate

For the filling

150g (5oz) dark chocolate, roughly chopped

100g (3½oz) butter

3 tbsp double cream

Start by making the filling. Melt the chocolate, butter and cream together in a heatproof bowl set over a saucepan of barely simmering water, making sure the surface of the water does not touch the bowl. Stir well until smooth, then leave to cool until thickened and a piping consistency but not hard.

Meanwhile, make the macaroons. Line 4 baking sheets with baking paper. Put the icing sugar, ground almonds and cocoa powder into a food processor and grind to a very fine powder. Sift the powder into a bowl.

In a separate, clean, dry bowl, whisk the egg whites to soft peaks, adding the caster sugar a little at a time. Just before the whites are peaking, add a point of a knife of red food colouring (to enhance the natural reddish colour of the cocoa powder). Using a rubber spatula, gradually fold the almond mixture into the egg whites until smooth and glossy but not runny.

Spoon the mixture into a piping bag fitted with a plain piping nozzle, then pipe discs about 3cm (1¼in) in diameter on to the prepared baking sheets. Leave to stand for 15 minutes at room temperature to allow the tops to start to dry. (In France, this is called *croutage*.) Meanwhile, preheat the oven to 150°C (fan 130°C)/300°F/gas mark 2.

Bake in the oven for 20 minutes, or until the baking paper peels off easily from the macaroons. Leave to cool completely on the baking sheets, then remove them from the baking paper.

When the macaroons are cold, spoon the filling into a piping bag, then pipe some ganache on to the base of a macaroon. Sandwich together with a second macaroon. Repeat with the remaining macaroons. Scatter with finely chopped dark chocolate to decorate before serving. Store the macaroons in airtight containers for up to a few days. It is best not to put them in the refrigerator, as this makes them sticky.

Salted butter caramel cake

As you may know, I am a great fan of salted butter caramel and after lots of experiments I've come up with this delicious recipe, which is made of layers of salted butter caramel biscuit baked into a rich and dark chocolate cake. A winning recipe.

Serves 8–10

Preparation time: 35 minutes, plus chilling and cooling

Cooking time: 45 minutes

200g (7oz) dark chocolate, roughly chopped

100g (3½oz) unsalted butter, plus extra for greasing

150ml (¼ pint) milk

4 eggs, separated

125g (4oz) golden caster sugar

100g (3½oz) plain flour

pinch of sea salt crystals, to decorate

For the caramel biscuit

225g (7½oz) digestive biscuits

300g (10oz) golden caster sugar

2 tbsp water

100ml (3½fl oz) single cream

100g (3½oz) salted butter, plus extra for greasing

2 pinches of sea salt

For the chocolate glaze

200g (7oz) dark chocolate, chopped

200ml (7fl oz) single cream

First make the caramel biscuit. Grease 2 x 22cm (8½in) diameter sandwich cake tins and line the bases with baking paper.

Put the biscuits into a food processor and whizz to fine crumbs. Put the sugar and water into a heavy-based saucepan and dissolve over a low heat. Increase the heat and cook until it forms an amber caramel. Remove from the heat and carefully stir in the cream, followed by the butter and salt. Stir the biscuit crumbs into the caramel, then divide equally between the prepared tins and press down with the back of a spoon. Place in the freezer to set.

To make the sponge, preheat the oven to 180°C (fan 160°C)/350°F/ gas mark 4. Grease a deep 22cm (8½in) diameter loose-bottomed cake tin and line with baking paper.

Melt the chocolate, butter and milk together in a heatproof bowl set over a saucepan of barely simmering water, making sure the surface of the water does not touch the bowl.

In a large bowl, whisk the egg yolks and sugar together using an electric hand whisk until pale and fluffy. Stir in the chocolate mixture, then fold in the flour. In a clean, dry bowl, whisk the egg whites to soft peaks, then gently fold into the chocolate mixture.

Remove the caramel biscuit discs from the freezer and remove them from the tins, discarding the lining paper. Place one of the discs on the bottom of the prepared loose-bottomed cake tin and spread with half of the cake mixture. Lay the other biscuit disc on top and cover with the remaining cake mixture.

Bake in the oven for 25–30 minutes until the cake is just cooked – it should be almost undercooked for extra gooeyness. Leave to cool in the tin for 10 minutes, then turn out on to a cooling rack to cool completely.

To make the glaze, put the chocolate into a heatproof bowl. Put the cream into a saucepan and heat to simmering point, then pour one-quarter over the chocolate. Leave for 1 minute until the chocolate starts to melt, then gently stir in the rest of the cream until smooth and glossy.

Cover the cooled cake with the chocolate glaze and use a palette knife to spread it evenly over the top and down the side. Lightly sprinkle sea salt crystals on top of the cake, then chill it in the refrigerator until set before serving.

Swiss walnut and chocolate cake

I used to make this recipe when I was a kid. I'm not too sure where the Swiss origin comes from, but even today it is still one of my all-time favourite cakes to make, as I love the combination of walnuts and chocolate.

Serves 8

Preparation time: 15 minutes, plus cooling

Cooking time: 40–45 minutes

100g (3½oz) dark chocolate, roughly chopped

150g (5oz) unsalted butter, softened, plus extra for greasing

150g (5oz) golden caster sugar

2 eggs

75g (3oz) plain flour

2 tsp baking powder

2 tsp vanilla paste or extract

65g (2½oz) roasted and chopped walnuts (see Tip below)

icing sugar, for dusting

50g walnut halves, to decorate

Preheat the oven to 180°C (fan 160°C)/350°F/gas mark 4. Grease a 22cm (8½in) diameter cake tin and line with baking paper.

Melt the chocolate in a heatproof bowl set over a saucepan of barely simmering water, making sure the surface of the water does not touch the bowl. Leave to cool for a few minutes.

In a large bowl, cream the butter and sugar together until pale and fluffy. Beat in the eggs one at the time. Sift the flour and baking powder together, then carefully fold in. Add the cooled chocolate and the vanilla, then fold in the chopped walnuts.

Spoon the mixture into the prepared tin. Arrange the extra walnut halves on top in a circular pattern and bake in the oven for 30–35 minutes, or until a skewer inserted into the centre comes out clean – the texture will be very similar to a brownie.

Leave to cool in the tin for 10 minutes, then remove from the tin and transfer to a cooling rack. Serve dusted with icing sugar. A hot crème anglaise is perfect as an accompaniment.

Tip

For roasted walnuts or any other nuts, simply spread whole nuts over a baking tray and roast in the oven at 180°C (fan 160°C)/350°F/gas mark 4 for 8–10 minutes, or until golden and crisp – be sure to watch them, as they can burn quickly. Leave to cool, then chop.

White chocolate and peach melba muffins

Theses muffins are the perfect summer Sunday brunch as they are so delightfully fruity, fresh and yummy. My favourite and hopefully yours once tasted…

Makes 12
Preparation time: 15 minutes
Cooking time: 25 minutes

300g (10oz) plain flour
2 tsp baking powder
1 egg
150g (5oz) golden caster sugar
1 tsp vanilla extract or paste
225ml (7½fl oz) milk
50g (2oz) unsalted butter, melted and cooled
100g (3½oz) chopped peaches, fresh or canned
125g (4oz) white chocolate, cut into small chunks
100g (3½oz) fresh raspberries
icing sugar, for dusting

Preheat the oven to 180°C (fan 160°C)/350°F/ gas mark 4. Line a 12-hole muffin tin with paper muffin cases.

Sift the flour and baking powder into a bowl. In a separate bowl, beat the egg and sugar together using an electric hand whisk, then whisk in the vanilla, milk and cooled melted butter. Using a rubber spatula or metal spoon, fold the wet ingredients into the dry ingredients until the mixture is smooth, but don't over-mix. Briefly fold in the peaches and white chocolate.

Divide the mixture between the muffin cases, filling them three-quarters full. Bake in the oven for 25 minutes, or until a skewer inserted into the centres comes out clean. Leave to cool on a cooling rack.

In a small bowl, roughly crush the raspberries with a fork. Spoon them on top of the muffins just before serving. Decorate with a dusting of icing sugar.

Chocolate and pistachio biscotti

Originally from Italy, biscotti now adorn coffee shops across the world — they are the perfect combination with good coffee. These chocolate and pistachio ones are to die for…

Makes 26

Preparation time: 20 minutes, plus cooling

Cooking time: 50–55 minutes

100g (3½oz) unsalted butter, softened, plus extra for greasing

200g (7oz) golden caster sugar

2 eggs

275g (9oz) plain flour, plus extra for dusting

50g (2oz) cocoa powder

1 tsp bicarbonate of soda

125g (4oz) shelled pistachio nuts

75g (3oz) dark chocolate chips

Preheat the oven to 180°C (fan 160°C)/350°F/gas mark 4. Lightly grease 2 large baking sheets.

In a large bowl, cream the butter and sugar together until pale and fluffy. Beat in the eggs one at a time, then sift the flour, cocoa powder and bicarbonate of soda together and fold in. Gently stir in the pistachios and chocolate chips.

Turn the mixture out on to a floured surface and form into a large, slightly flattened loaf shape, about 30 x 7cm (12 x 3in). Carefully transfer to one of the prepared baking sheets and bake for 30 minutes. Remove from the oven and leave to cool for 10 minutes. Reduce the oven temperature to 150°C (fan 130°C)/300°F/gas mark 2.

Place the warm loaf on a chopping board and slice into 1cm (½in) thick slices. Arrange them on the baking sheets and return to the oven for a further 20–25 minutes, or until dry and crispy. Once cooked, transfer to a cooling rack to cool and harden.

You can store the biscotti in airtight containers for up to 2 weeks. They also make really nice presents when wrapped in a gift bag.

Chocolate florentines

These little treats are great as a gift when boxed or bagged beautifully and they make a great accompaniment for after-dinner coffee.

Makes 8

Preparation time: 20 minutes, plus cooling and setting

Cooking time: 8 minutes

50g (2oz) unsalted butter, softened, plus extra for greasing

50g (2oz) light muscovado sugar

2 tbsp plain flour

25g (1oz) toasted flaked almonds

25g (1oz) chopped hazelnuts, roasted (see Tip on page 44)

25g (1oz) chopped walnuts, roasted (see Tip on page 44)

50g (2oz) mixed peel

150g (5oz) milk chocolate, roughly chopped

Preheat the oven to 180°C (fan 160°C)/350°F/ gas mark 4. Grease a baking sheet or 10cm (4in) silicone florentine moulds.

In a bowl, cream the butter and sugar together until pale and fluffy. Sift in the flour, then fold in all the nuts and the peel.

Place 8 heaped spoonfuls of the mixture on the prepared baking sheet, leaving enough space between each to expand, or fill the moulds. Bake in the oven for about 6–7 minutes, or until the florentines are golden. Leave to cool on the baking sheet or in the moulds until cold.

Melt the chocolate in a heatproof bowl set over a saucepan of barely simmering water, making sure the surface of the water does not touch the bowl. Using a pastry brush, coat the base of each florentine with the melted chocolate. Before the chocolate sets, create waves in the chocolate using a fork, then place, chocolate side up, on baking paper to set at room temperature. Store in a cool, dry place for up to 2 weeks.

Tip

To vary the flavours, replace the nuts with shelled pistachios, pine nuts or glacé cherries.

Chocolate rum and raisin loaf

I usually keep the combination of rum and raisin for ice cream, but I will always make an exception for this very tasty loaf, as it is really the perfect combination and texture.

Serves 8

Preparation time: 25 minutes, plus soaking overnight and cooling

Cooking time: 50 minutes

100g (3½oz) unsalted butter, plus extra for greasing

150g (5oz) dark chocolate, roughly chopped

4 eggs, separated

200g (7oz) golden caster sugar

50g (2oz) ground almonds

100g (3½oz) plain flour

1 tbsp baking powder

For the rum and raisin ganache

75g (3oz) raisins

3 tbsp dark rum

175ml (6fl oz) single cream

25g (1oz) golden caster sugar

350g (11½oz) dark chocolate, chopped

25g (1oz) unsalted butter, softened

For the rum and raisin ganache, put the raisins and rum into a small bowl and leave to soak overnight.

Preheat the oven to 180°C (fan 160°C)/350°F/ gas mark 4. Grease a 900g (2lb) loaf tin and line with baking paper.

To make the cake, melt the butter and chocolate together in a heatproof bowl set over a saucepan of barely simmering water, making sure the surface of the water does not touch the bowl. Leave to cool for a few minutes.

In a large bowl, beat the egg yolks and sugar together using an electric hand whisk until pale and creamy. Add the cooled chocolate mixture with the ground almonds. Sift the flour and baking powder together, then beat in. In a large, clean, dry bowl, whisk the egg whites to stiff peaks, then gently fold into the mixture.

Spoon the mixture into the prepared tin and bake in the oven for 45 minutes, or until a skewer inserted into the centre comes out clean. Leave to cool in the tin for 5–10 minutes, then turn out on to a cooling rack to cool completely.

To make the rum and raisin ganache, put the cream and sugar into a saucepan and heat until steaming hot, but do not let it boil. Remove from the heat and add the chocolate, stirring until smooth and glossy. Gently stir in the butter, then fold in the soaked raisins.

To glaze the cake, place the cake on a cooling rack set over a large plate or baking tray. Spread the warm ganache all over the cake and smooth it evenly using a palette knife. Lift carefully on to a serving plate before the ganache sets. I like to sprinkle shredded gold leaf over the glossy cake for a touch of glamour!

Chocolate financiers with citrus crumble

Financiers have been around for hundreds of years. These soft, classic petits fours are mostly made of ground nuts, such as almonds or hazelnuts – the addition of chocolate and the zesty topping make this version really special.

Makes 24
Preparation time: 20 minutes
Cooking time: 12–15 minutes

40g (1½oz) dark chocolate, roughly chopped
75g (3oz) unsalted butter, softened, plus extra for greasing
50g (2oz) ground almonds
125g (4oz) golden icing sugar
40g (1½oz) plain flour
4 egg whites
grated lemon zest, to decorate

For the citrus crumble
25g (1oz) unsalted butter
finely grated zest of 1 lemon
2 drops of lemon extract
25g (1oz) plain flour
25g (1oz) golden icing sugar
50g (2oz) ground almonds

Preheat the oven to 180°C (fan 160°C)/350°F/gas mark 4. Lightly grease 2 x 12-hole silicone financier moulds or mini muffin trays.

First make the citrus crumble topping. Put the butter into a bowl and mix in the lemon zest and extract. Add all the remaining ingredients and rub in using your fingertips until the mixture resembles fine breadcrumbs. Put to one side.

Melt the chocolate and butter together in a heatproof bowl set over a saucepan of barely simmering water, making sure the surface of the water does not touch the bowl. Leave to cool for a few minutes.

Mix the ground almonds, icing sugar and flour into the cooled chocolate mixture. In a large, clean, dry bowl, whisk the egg whites to soft peaks, then gently fold into the chocolate mixture.

Divide the mixture between the holes of the trays, filling them three-quarters full. Generously sprinkle the citrus crumble over the tops and bake in the oven for 10–12 minutes. Leave to cool in the trays for 5 minutes, then transfer to a cooling rack. Sprinkle with grated lemon zest to decorate before serving.

If you manage not to eat them all immediately, any remaining financiers will freeze well.

Chocolate waffles

As kids, we used to love going to Belgium for two reasons – first, the light, fluffy waffle, and second, the famous chocolate. This is my homage to these great trips – a combination of both waffle and chocolate.

Makes 12–16

Preparation time: 5 minutes

Cooking time: 5 minutes per waffle

50g (2oz) cocoa powder

2 tsp ground cinnamon

250g (8oz) butter, melted

300g (10oz) golden caster sugar

4 eggs, beaten

250g (8oz) plain flour

2 tbsp milk

2 tsp vanilla paste or extract

icing sugar and cocoa powder, for dusting

Preheat a waffle iron. Sift the cocoa powder into a large bowl and stir in the cinnamon and melted butter. Add the sugar, eggs and flour, then whisk in the milk and vanilla until smooth.

Fill the waffle iron with some of the mixture and cook according to the manufacturer's instructions. Repeat until all the mixture is used.

Dust the waffles with icing sugar and cocoa powder and serve warm. These are great served with one of the chocolate sauces on pages 168–9.

Breton shortbread with chocolate

Every pâtisserie or bakery in my birth region of Brittany will have this speciality in their display … and each one will keep its recipe a secret! Here, I am sharing my grandmother Camille's recipe.

Serves 8
Preparation time: 15 minutes
Cooking time: 40–45 minutes

350g (11½oz) plain flour
250g (8oz) golden caster sugar
250g (8oz) slightly salted butter, cubed, plus extra for greasing
6 egg yolks
2 tbsp dark rum
2 tsp vanilla extract
150g (5oz) dark chocolate chips

Preheat the oven to 180°C (fan 160°C)/350°F/gas mark 4. Grease a 24cm (9½in) diameter flan tin and line the base with baking paper.

Put the flour and sugar into a bowl and mix together. Add the butter and rub in using your fingertips until the mixture resembles fine breadcrumbs. In a separate bowl, beat 5 of the egg yolks with the rum and vanilla extract, then mix into the dry ingredients. Stir in the chocolate chips.

Spread the mixture into the prepared tin. Beat the remaining egg yolk, then brush over the top. Using a fork, make a crisscross design across the top.

Bake in the oven for 40–45 minutes, or until golden and cooked through. Leave to cool in the tin for a few minutes, then carefully turn out on to a cooling rack to cool completely.

Chocolate shortbreads

For over ten years I was a member of the beautiful Skibo Castle in Scotland. These chocolate shortbreads were always one of the highlights of the trip to this retreat.

Makes 18

Preparation time: 15 minutes, plus chilling

Cooking time: 10–12 minutes

150g (5oz) slightly salted butter, softened, plus extra for greasing

125g (4oz) light muscovado sugar

2 tsp vanilla paste or extract

175g (6oz) plain flour

25g (1oz) cocoa powder

150g (5oz) dark chocolate chips

40g (1½oz) golden caster sugar

In a large bowl, cream the butter, muscovado sugar and vanilla together until pale and fluffy. Sift the flour and cocoa powder together, fold in and combine to form a crumbly dough. Stir in the chocolate chips.

Sprinkle the caster sugar on to a clean work surface. Form the dough into a 5cm (2in) diameter sausage, then roll in the sugar to coat. Cover with clingfilm and leave to rest in the refrigerator for at least 2 hours.

Preheat the oven to 180°C (fan 160°C)/350°F/ gas mark 4. Grease 2 large baking sheets.

Using a large knife, cut the dough into 1cm (½in) thick discs and place on the prepared baking sheets. Bake in the oven for 10–12 minutes, or until the edges are firm to the touch. Leave to cool on the sheets, then store in an airtight tin or cookie jar for up to 1 week.

Crispy malted chocolate meringues

I've always been a huge fan of meringues, but they need to dry out properly to achieve a lovely crunch and a chewy centre. The addition of the malt powder and the sexy swirls of chocolate make these super-special.

Makes 6
Preparation time: 15 minutes, plus cooling
Cooking time: 2 hours 5 minutes

150g (5oz) dark chocolate, roughly chopped
3 egg whites
100g (3½oz) golden caster sugar
100g (3½oz) golden icing sugar
20g (¾oz) cocoa powder
15g (½oz) malt powder

Preheat the oven to 110°C (fan 90°C)/225°F/gas mark ¼. Line 2 baking sheets with baking paper.

Melt the chocolate in a heatproof bowl set over a saucepan of barely simmering water, making sure the surface of the water does not touch the bowl.

In a clean, dry bowl, whisk the egg whites using an electric hand whisk to soft peaks. Add the caster sugar a little at a time, whisking continuously until the mixture is glossy. Sift the icing sugar, cocoa powder and malt powder together, then fold into the egg whites using a rubber spatula. Gently swirl the melted chocolate into the meringue mixture to form a marbled effect.

Spoon the meringue into 6 large dollops on the prepared baking sheets (I like mine to be slightly misshapen) and place in the oven for 2 hours, then turn the oven off and leave the meringues inside to cool completely.

When cold, remove from the baking paper and store in airtight containers for up to 1 week. I like to serve these meringues piled high with unsweetened whipped cream and a generous dusting of grated dark chocolate.

Tip

Always use a clean, dry bowl to whisk egg whites, as any trace of grease will prevent perfect peaks from forming.

Chocolate Kouglof

Alsace and the east of France are very famous for their baking and cooking. The Kouglof is a traditional recipe baked in a very characteristic-shaped mould. As well as looking good it tastes divine.

Serves 8–10

Preparation time: 35 minutes, plus soaking and chilling overnight, and rising and cooling

Cooking time: 50–55 minutes

75g (3oz) golden sultanas

100ml (3½fl oz) Cognac

20g (¾oz) dried yeast

100g (3½oz) golden caster sugar

100ml (3½fl oz) lukewarm milk

500g (1lb) plain flour, plus extra for dusting

2 pinches of salt

3 eggs

200g (7oz) unsalted butter, cubed, plus extra for greasing

75g (3oz) almonds, chopped

2 tbsp mixed peel

100g (3½oz) dark chocolate chips

For the glaze

150g (5oz) dark chocolate, roughly chopped

50g (2oz) unsalted butter

2 tbsp icing sugar

Put the sultanas and brandy into a bowl and leave to soak overnight at room temperature.

The following day, put the yeast, sugar and milk in a separate bowl and mix gently to dissolve. Leave to stand for 10 minutes.

Sift the flour and salt into the bowl of a freestanding mixer fitted with a dough hook. Add the eggs and yeast mixture and mix together for 10 minutes, or until the dough comes away from the side of the bowl. Add the butter a little at a time until well incorporated. Add the remaining ingredients, including the soaked sultanas, and mix for a further 5 minutes.

Grease and flour a 2 litre (3½ pint) kouglof mould. Push the dough into it, cover with clingfilm and chill in the refrigerator overnight. The following day, remove the mould from the refrigerator and leave the dough to rise for 4–5 hours at room temperature.

Bake the kouglof in a preheated oven, 170°C (fan 150°C)/ 325°F/gas mark 3, for 45–50 minutes, or until golden. Turn out of the mould on to a cooling rack and leave to cool completely.

To make the glaze, melt the chocolate and butter together in a heatproof bowl set over a saucepan of barely simmering water, making sure the surface of the water does not touch the bowl. When melted, fold in the sugar. Pour the glaze over the top of the cake and leave to set. Traditionally, this cake is served with beaten crème fraîche.

Chocolate, pumpkin and pecan cake

I'd describe this cake as a perfect winter warmer, full of very earthy flavours and a spicy, nutty crunch. It's best eaten a day after baking.

Serves 8
Preparation time: 20 minutes, plus cooling and resting overnight
Cooking time: 1 hour 25 minutes

125g (4oz) pecan nuts

1 tsp cayenne pepper

225g (7½oz) dark chocolate, roughly chopped

150g (5oz) unsalted butter, plus extra for greasing 3 eggs

275g (9oz) dark muscovado sugar

275ml (9fl oz) water

3 tsp vanilla paste or extract

250g (8oz) self-raising flour

3 tsp ground cinnamon

100g (3½oz) peeled, deseeded pumpkin, grated

cocoa powder, for dusting

Preheat the oven to 170°C (fan 150°C)/325°F/ gas mark 3. Grease a 23cm (9in) diameter springform cake tin and line with baking paper.

In a large bowl, mix the pecans and cayenne pepper together. Place the nuts on a baking sheet and roast in the oven for 10 minutes, or until they are golden and crunchy. Leave to cool, then roughly chop.

Melt the chocolate and butter together in a heatproof bowl set over a saucepan of barely simmering water, making sure the surface of the water does not touch the bowl.

Beat the eggs and sugar together in a bowl until nice and smooth, then beat in the melted chocolate mixture, followed by the water and vanilla. Sift the flour and cinnamon together, then fold in until smooth. Fold in the pumpkin and chopped pecans.

Spoon the mixture into the prepared tin and bake in the oven for 1 hour 10 minutes, or until a skewer inserted into the centre comes out clean. Leave to cool in the tin for 10 minutes, then turn out on to a cooling rack to cool completely.

Wrap the cake in clingfilm and store at room temperature for at least 24 hours before eating. Dust with cocoa powder before serving.

Apricot and chocolate charlotte

Desserts & Puddings

Apricot and chocolate charlotte

This was my mum's favourite recipe. She used to make this spectacular dessert on Sunday when we had guests. It has to be made the day before, which makes your life easier on the day if you are entertaining.

Serves 6

Preparation time: 30 minutes, plus cooling and chilling overnight

Cooking time: 15 minutes

butter, for greasing

30–35 sponge finger biscuits

For the apricots

50ml (2fl oz) water

100g (3½oz) golden caster sugar

300g (10oz) fresh apricots, stoned and diced

juice of 1 lemon

5g (¼oz) unsalted butter

2 tsp clear honey

1 tbsp apricot preserve

2 tsp balsamic vinegar

For the chocolate mousse

100g (3½oz) dark chocolate, roughly chopped

25g (1oz) unsalted butter

3 tbsp crème fraîche

2 egg yolks

100g (3½oz) egg whites

15g (½oz) golden caster sugar

Start with the apricots. Put the water and sugar into a saucepan and heat gently until the sugar has dissolved. Put the apricots into a heatproof bowl, then pour over the syrup and add the lemon juice. Leave to cool, then drain the apricots, reserving the syrup.

Melt the butter in a small frying pan. Add the apricots and fry until golden. Remove from the heat and add the honey, apricot preserve and vinegar. Return to the heat and cook for a further 2 minutes, then leave to cool.

For the chocolate mousse, melt the chocolate and butter together in a heatproof bowl set over a saucepan of barely simmering water, making sure the surface of the water does not touch the bowl. Remove from the heat and fold in the crème fraîche first, then the egg yolks. In a clean, dry bowl, whisk the egg whites and sugar to stiff peaks, then gently fold into the chocolate mixture to form a lovely smooth mousse.

To make the charlotte, lightly grease a 15cm (6in) diameter charlotte mould and line the base with baking paper. Dip the sponge fingers into the reserved apricot syrup, then use to carefully line the charlotte mould, making sure they are tightly placed.

Spoon one-third of the chocolate mousse over the base, spoon over half of the cooled apricots, then cover with a layer of dipped sponge fingers. Repeat the layers, finishing with a layer of sponge fingers. If necessary, trim off any excess sponge from around the edge to level the top. Cover the top with greaseproof paper and place a few small plates on top as weights. Leave to chill in the refrigerator overnight.

One hour before serving, turn the charlotte out on to a serving plate and leave to stand at room temperature. Decorate with any leftover apricots and serve with crème fraîche. See previous page for the finished result.

1. Fry the apricots in honey, apricot preserve and balsamic vinegar.

2. Whisk the egg whites, then fold them into the melted chocolate mixture.

3. Grease and line the base of a charlotte mould, then line with sponge fingers.

4. Spoon some of the chocolate mixture into the base, then add half of the apricots.

5. Add a layer of sponge fingers dipped in the apricot syrup.

6. Repeat the chocolate and apricot layers, finishing with a layer of sponge fingers. Cover, then weight down the top and chill in the refrigerator before turning out.

Chocolate petits pots

If you like a small treat at the end of a meal, this recipe is for you.
It's a classic you will find in most French bistros and because of its
size it won't make you feel too guilty.

Serves 8
Preparation time: 10 minutes,
plus cooling and chilling
Cooking time: 5 minutes

1 litre (1¾ pints) milk

200g (7oz) dark chocolate,
roughly chopped

50g (2oz) light muscovado sugar

75g (3oz) cornflour

50g (2oz) unsalted butter,
cut into small cubes

2 tsp brandy

Reserve 150ml (¼ pint) of the milk and pour the
remainder into a small saucepan. Add the chocolate
and sugar and heat gently, stirring until the sugar has
completely dissolved.

Blend the cornflour with the reserved milk in a bowl
using a small balloon whisk, then stir into the chocolate
milk and bring to the boil, stirring continuously.
Remove from the heat and add the butter, then stir
in the brandy.

Pour into 8 small cups or ramekin dishes. Leave to cool,
then leave to set in the refrigerator for at least 4 hours.
Remove from the refrigerator 1 hour before serving.

Tip

To vary the flavour, substitute the brandy with orange
liqueur, kirsch, cassis or framboise.

Gâteau Concorde

This recipe was created by the godfather of modern pâtisserie, Gaston Lenôtre. If you like chocolate and meringue this is cake heaven!

Serves 8

Preparation time: 40 minutes, plus cooling and chilling

Cooking time: 1 hour 35 minutes

125g (4oz) dark chocolate, roughly chopped

75g (3oz) unsalted butter

3 egg yolks

5 egg whites

icing sugar and cocoa powder, for dusting

For the meringues

5 egg whites

175g (6oz) golden caster sugar

150g (5oz) icing sugar

35g (1¼oz) cocoa powder

First make the meringues. Preheat the oven to 150°C (fan 130°C)/300°F/gas mark 2. Line 4 baking sheets with baking paper, then draw a 22cm (8½in) diameter disc on 3 of the papers.

In a large, clean, dry bowl, whisk the egg whites to stiff peaks, adding the caster sugar a little at a time. Sift the icing sugar and cocoa powder together, then gently fold into the meringue mixture.

Spoon the mixture into a piping bag fitted with a 1cm (½in) diameter plain piping nozzle, then pipe the mixture on to the 3 marked discs on the baking paper. Using the remaining mixture, pipe long, thin lengths of meringue on the remaining baking sheet. Bake all the meringues in the oven for 1 hour 30 minutes until very crisp. Remove from the oven and leave to cool.

Next make a chocolate mousse. Melt the chocolate in a heatproof bowl set over a saucepan of barely simmering water, making sure the surface of the water does not touch the bowl. Remove from the heat and stir in the butter, then the egg yolks. In a large, clean, dry bowl, whisk the egg whites to soft peaks, then gently fold in the chocolate mixture. Cover and chill in the refrigerator for a few minutes until set enough to pipe.

To assemble the cake, spoon just over half of the chocolate mousse into a piping bag fitted with a 1cm (½in) diameter plain piping nozzle, then pipe a little of the mousse on to a serving plate to secure one of the meringue discs on top. Pipe the mousse all over the meringue, then place another disc on top, gently pressing down to secure. Pipe another layer of mousse on top, then place the remaining disc, upside down, on top to give a flat surface. Using a palette knife, spread the remaining mousse over the top and sides.

Cut the lengths of meringue into 2cm (¾in) pieces with a sharp knife, then randomly place over the cake until it is completely covered. Cover with clingfilm and chill in the refrigerator for at least 4 hours. To serve, dust with icing sugar, then a slight dusting of cocoa powder.

Tip

Make the meringues the day before serving so that they are really dry.

Chocolate and tonka bean crème brûlées

Tonka beans are sweet and deliciously perfumed with vanilla and rich milk chocolate. This strong spice adds a touch of suave luxury to the brûlées.

Serves 6

Preparation time: 15 minutes, plus chilling overnight

Cooking time: 1 hour 10 minutes

100g (3½oz) dark chocolate, finely chopped
1 tonka bean
600ml (1 pint) double cream
8 egg yolks
75g (3oz) golden caster sugar
4 tbsp demerara sugar

Preheat the oven to 110°C (fan 90°C)/225°F/gas mark ¼. Place 6 brûlée dishes or flameproof ramekins into a shallow roasting tin and fill the tin with water to come halfway up the sides of the dishes.

Put the chocolate into a heatproof bowl. Using a nutmeg grater, grate the tonka bean, then mix with the chocolate. Put the cream into a saucepan and heat to just below boiling point, then pour over the chocolate and mix gently until the chocolate has melted.

In a separate bowl, whisk the egg yolks and caster sugar together using an electric hand whisk until pale and fluffy. Whisk the chocolate cream a little at a time into the egg mixture.

Pour into the dishes in the bain-marie and bake in the oven for 1 hour, or until set.

Leave to cool, then chill in the refrigerator overnight.

To serve, sprinkle demerara sugar over the top of each crème, then caramelize using a kitchen blowtorch.

Tip

If you do not have a kitchen blowtorch, sprinkle the crème brûlées with the sugar and put on a baking sheet. Place under a hot grill until the sugar caramelizes.

Raspberry and chocolate tart

As well as the great combination of dark chocolate and raspberries, the addition of the chocolate shortcrust pastry gives a three-dimensional taste and texture to this yummy recipe.

Serves 6

Preparation time: 25 minutes, plus chilling and cooling

Cooking time: 25 minutes

175g (6oz) plain flour, plus extra for dusting

50g (2oz) cocoa powder

50g (2oz) golden icing sugar

150g (5oz) unsalted butter, cubed, plus extra for greasing

3 egg yolks

1 tsp vanilla extract

500g (1lb) raspberries

icing sugar, for dusting

For the ganache

200g (7oz) dark chocolate, roughly chopped

200ml (7fl oz) single cream

2 tsp vanilla extract

75g (3oz) unsalted butter

Sift the flour, cocoa powder and icing sugar together into a large bowl. Add the butter and rub in using your fingertips until the mixture resembles fine breadcrumbs. Add the egg yolks and gently mix together, then add the vanilla and combine to form a smooth dough. Cover with clingfilm and leave to rest in the refrigerator for at least 30 minutes.

Preheat the oven to 190°C (fan 170°C)/375°F/gas mark 5. Lightly grease a 24cm (9½in) diameter tart tin.

Roll out the pastry on a lightly floured surface and carefully use to line the tin. Cover with ovenproof clingfilm and prick a few holes to avoid pockets of air while it bakes. Fill the pastry case with baking beans and bake in the oven for 15 minutes. Remove the clingfilm and beans and return to the oven for a further 5 minutes. Leave to cool.

To make the ganache, melt the chocolate in a heatproof bowl set over a saucepan of barely simmering water, making sure the surface of the water does not touch the bowl. Meanwhile, put the cream into a saucepan and heat until steaming hot, but do not let it boil. Remove the melted chocolate from the heat and slowly pour in the cream, gently stirring the mixture. Add the vanilla, then the butter and stir together.

Pack the cooled pastry case with raspberries, saving a few for decoration. Pour the hot chocolate ganache over the raspberries to fill to the top of the pastry. Leave to set in the refrigerator for at least 30 minutes. Serve decorated with the reserved raspberries dusted with a little icing sugar.

Pear and chocolate clafoutis

Clafoutis is a very rustic dish usually made with cherries. This dessert has had a bit of a revival and you will love this combination. I make it with raw pears to give a nice crunch.

Serves 6

Preparation time: 20 minutes, plus chilling

Cooking time: 25–30 minutes

unsalted butter, for greasing

1 tbsp muscovado sugar

250g (8oz) dark chocolate, roughly chopped

50g (2oz) plain flour

1 tsp ground cinnamon

4 eggs

50ml (2fl oz) whipping cream

200ml (7fl oz) milk

4 ripe pears, peeled, cored and thickly sliced

Preheat the oven to 180°C (fan 160°C)/350°F/gas mark 4. Grease a 1.5 litre (2½ pint) ceramic gratin dish and sprinkle with the sugar.

Melt the chocolate in a heatproof bowl set over a saucepan of barely simmering water, making sure the surface of the water does not touch the bowl.

Sift the flour and cinnamon together into a bowl, then beat in the eggs, cream and milk to form a batter. Stir in the melted chocolate, then pour it into the prepared dish. Sprinkle the pears all over the chocolate custard, letting them sink.

Bake in the oven for 20–25 minutes, or until set. Leave to cool completely in the dish, then chill in the refrigerator before serving.

Chocolate and blackberry mille feuille

You can't beat the lightness, flakiness and buttery texture of a good mille feuille. The combination of the cassis and blackberries makes this version very sophisticated.

Serves 8

Preparation time: 30 minutes, plus cooling

Cooking time: 20–30 minutes

500g (1lb) ready-made all-butter puff pastry

plain flour, for dusting

25g (1oz) cocoa powder

400g (13oz) blackberries

icing sugar and cocoa powder, for dusting

For the chocolate cream

100g (3½oz) dark chocolate, chopped

100ml (3½fl oz) single cream

450ml (¾ pint) whipping cream

2 tbsp crème de cassis, plus extra for drizzling

Preheat the oven to 220°C (fan 200°C)/425°F/gas mark 7. Roll out the pastry on a lightly floured surface to a large rectangle and sift over half of the cocoa powder. Fold one end of the rectangle into the centre and repeat with the opposite end, so that each end meets in the middle. Repeat the process, adding another dusting of cocoa powder, then roll out the pastry to a thin rectangle, about 34 x 28cm (13½ x 11in).

Place the pastry on a large baking sheet and trim to fit if necessary. Prick the pastry all over with a fork, cover with a sheet of greaseproof paper and weight the pastry down with a second baking sheet.

Bake in the oven for 10–15 minutes, or until the pastry begins to colour. Remove the top baking sheet and greaseproof paper, then return to the oven for a further 5–10 minutes, or until cooked. Leave to cool.

Meanwhile, make the chocolate cream. Put the chocolate into a large heatproof bowl. Put the single cream into a saucepan and heat to just below boiling point. Pour the cream on to the chocolate, stirring gently until smooth. Leave to cool. Whip the whipping cream to soft peaks. Mix the cooled chocolate mixture into the whipped cream, then fold in the crème de cassis.

To assemble, cut the cooled pastry into 16 small rectangles. Using a piping bag or palette knife, pipe or spread a thick layer of the chocolate cream on to all the pastry rectangles. Arrange the blackberries on half of the rectangles, reserving 8 for decoration, then add a little more chocolate cream between the berries. Sandwich the cream-covered pastry rectangles on top of the berries and dust with icing sugar and cocoa powder.

Cut the reserved berries in half, drizzle with cassis and use to decorate the mille feuille.

Gâteau opéra

This is another great French classic that you will find in pâtisserie windows all over France. It's also one of the bestsellers at my London cake boutique.

Serves 8

Preparation time: 1 hour, plus cooling and chilling

Cooking time: 25 minutes

3 egg whites

1 tbsp golden caster sugar

150g (5oz) ground almonds

150g (5oz) icing sugar

3 eggs

35g (1¼oz) plain flour

20g (¾oz) unsalted butter, melted

For the coffee buttercream

200g (7oz) golden caster sugar

2 tbsp water

½ tsp vanilla extract

1 egg, plus 1 egg yolk

200g (7oz) unsalted butter

2 tbsp espresso coffee, cooled

For the ganache

250g (8oz) dark chocolate, chopped

35g (1¼oz) unsalted butter, softened

125ml (4fl oz) double cream

125ml (4fl oz) milk

For the coffee syrup

50ml (2fl oz) espresso coffee

2 tbsp dark rum

1 tsp golden caster sugar

To decorate

50g (2oz) dark chocolate, chopped

50g (2oz) unsalted butter, melted

First make the sponge. Preheat the oven to 200°C (fan 180°C)/400°F/gas mark 6 and line 2 x 20 x 30cm (8 x 12in), 1cm (½in) deep baking trays with baking paper.

Use a freestanding mixer or electric hand whisk to whisk the egg whites and caster sugar to stiff peaks. In a separate bowl, mix together the almonds and icing sugar, then add the whole eggs and whisk again until pale and doubled in volume. Sift the flour and fold in, then gently fold in the egg whites followed by the melted butter. Divide the mixture between the baking trays, tilting the tins to spread the mixture evenly. Bake in the oven for 7–10 minutes until golden and springy to the touch – watch carefully, as the sponge cooks quickly. Turn out on to cooling racks and leave to cool.

To make the coffee buttercream, put the sugar and water into a saucepan and heat to 120°C (250°F) on a sugar thermometer, if you have one, or until syrupy and almost a caramel. Add the vanilla to the syrup once the mixture thickens, then remove from the heat. In a heatproof bowl, whisk the egg and egg yolk together using an electric hand whisk, then pour on the hot syrup with the beaters still running and continue to whisk until fluffy. Cool slightly, then beat in the butter. Stir in the coffee, then leave to cool.

To make the ganache, put the chocolate and butter into a heatproof bowl. Put the cream and milk into a saucepan and heat until steaming hot, then pass through a sieve on to the chocolate and butter. Stir until melted, smooth and thick. Leave to set for a few minutes to form a spreading consistency.

Using the base of a 20cm (8in) square cake tin as a stencil, cut out a square from the sponge. Repeat with the other sponge sheet, then join together the left-over sponge and cut out a third square.

To assemble the cake, fit the first sponge square in the bottom of a 20cm (8in) loose-bottomed cake tin, 8cm (3in) deep, then mix together the coffee syrup ingredients and brush over the sponge. Spread over half of the ganache, then add the sponge square made with the 2 halves. Brush again with coffee syrup, then spread over the coffee buttercream. Top with the final square, then brush with syrup and spread the remaining ganache over the top. Chill in the refrigerator for 30 minutes.

To decorate in the traditional French way, melt the dark chocolate in a bowl over a saucepan of barely simmering water, making sure the surface of the water does not touch the bowl. Stir in the melted butter, then spoon the chocolate into a small piping bag with a small hole snipped at the tip. Pipe the word 'Opéra' on top of the cake, then leave to set. You could also sprinkle over some gold leaf flakes for a luxurious touch, if you like. Remove the cake tin using a kitchen blowtorch or the heat of your hands.

Hot chocolate soufflés

I love soufflé. It is such a simple recipe with few ingredients, but it still has the wow factor every time you make one. This chocolate version, especially when served with a vanilla ice-cream drop, is superb.

Serves 6
Preparation time: 20 minutes
Cooking time: 15 minutes

unsalted butter, for greasing
125g (4oz) dark chocolate, roughly chopped
2 tsp dark rum (optional)
2 tbsp crème fraîche
4 eggs, separated, plus 2 egg whites
pinch of salt
icing sugar, for dusting

Preheat the oven to 200°C (fan 180°C)/400°F/ gas mark 6. Grease 6 ramekin dishes.

Melt the chocolate in a heatproof bowl set over a saucepan of barely simmering water, making sure the surface of the water does not touch the bowl. Stir in the rum, if using. Remove from the heat and add the crème fraîche, then the egg yolks.

In a large, clean, dry bowl, whisk all the egg whites and the salt to soft peaks.

Fold one-quarter of the egg whites into the chocolate mixture, then fold in the remaining whites.

Fill the prepared ramekins to the top with the mixture, then clean the rims using your finger and thumb. Place on a baking sheet and bake in the oven for 10–12 minutes, or until nicely risen. Dust with icing sugar and serve immediately.

Tip

For a delicious party trick, serve your soufflés with an ice-cream drop. Before you make the soufflés, scoop out 6 balls of good-quality vanilla ice cream and place on a freezer-proof plate. Keep in the freezer until ready to serve. When serving the soufflés at the table, drop an ice-cream ball into each soufflé.

Chocolate and banana tarte tatin

This is a great winter dessert and seriously indulgent. The chocolate, caramel-infused bananas are full of flavour and the delicate pastry simply melts in your mouth.

Serves 6
Preparation time: 15 minutes
Cooking time: 30–35 minutes

350g (11½oz) ready-made all-butter puff pastry

plain flour, for dusting

100g (3½oz) light muscovado sugar

50g (2oz) unsalted butter, plus extra for greasing

75g (3oz) dark chocolate, finely chopped

2 cinnamon sticks

5 firm bananas, cut into large chunks

Preheat the oven to 200°C (fan 180°C)/400°F/ gas mark 6. Grease a 22cm (8½in) diameter tarte tatin tin. Roll out the pastry on a floured surface to a disc 2.5cm (1in) larger than the tin. Put to one side.

Put the sugar and butter into the tin and cook gently over a medium heat until it forms a dark blond caramel. Remove from the heat and add the chocolate, stirring until melted. Drop the cinnamon sticks into the centre of the tin.

Arrange the banana chunks tightly in the tin. Place the pastry over the top, tucking in the overhanging pastry between the fruit and the tin. Using a small knife, pierce the top of the pastry to allow the steam to escape.

Bake in the oven for 25–30 minutes, or until the pastry is puffed up and golden. Invert on to a serving dish immediately. Serve with crème fraîche or ice cream.

Harlequin

I came across this recipe when working for chefs Michel and Albert Roux. It's a very delicate combination of dark and white chocolate with whisky and coconut. This is a great dessert and certainly worth the effort.

Serves 8
Preparation time: 1 hour, plus cooling and chilling overnight
Cooking time: 40–45 minutes

butter, for greasing
4 eggs
125g (4oz) golden caster sugar
25g (1oz) plain flour
25g (1oz) cocoa powder
4 tbsp toasted desiccated coconut
icing sugar, for dusting

For the white chocolate cream
50g (2oz) white chocolate, roughly chopped
125g (4oz) unsalted butter, softened
250g (8oz) icing sugar
1 tablespoon milk

For the dark chocolate cream
150g (5oz) dark chocolate, roughly chopped
300ml (½ pint) whipping cream

For the whisky syrup
50g (2oz) golden caster sugar
50ml (2fl oz) water
1 tbsp whisky

Preheat the oven to 180°C (fan 160°C)/350°F/gas mark 4. Lightly grease 2 x 20cm (8in) diameter sandwich cake tins and line with baking paper.

To make the sponge, separate 2 of the eggs and put the yolks and 2 whole eggs into a heatproof bowl with 100g (3½oz) of the sugar. Set the bowl over a saucepan of simmering water and whisk using a balloon whisk until the mixture reaches 40°C (104°F) on a sugar thermometer. Using an electric hand whisk, continue whisking the mixture until it doubles in volume. Sift the flour and cocoa powder together and then gently fold in.

In a clean, dry bowl, whisk the egg whites and the remaining sugar to soft peaks, then fold into the sponge mixture. Spoon into the prepared tins and bake in the oven for 20–25 minutes, or until a skewer inserted into the centres comes out clean. Turn out on to a cooling rack to cool.

To make the white chocolate cream, melt the white chocolate in a heatproof bowl set over a saucepan of barely simmering water, making sure the surface of the water does not touch the bowl. Leave to cool. Beat the butter and half of the icing sugar together until smooth, then add the remaining icing sugar a little at a time, beating until smooth. Stir in the cooled white chocolate, add the milk and beat for 2 minutes. Set aside.

For the dark chocolate cream, melt the dark chocolate as above. Meanwhile, whip the cream to soft peaks, then quickly whisk one-third into the hot melted chocolate. Gently fold in the remaining cream.

For the whisky syrup, heat the sugar and water in a saucepan until the sugar has dissolved. Boil for 4 minutes, then leave to cool before stirring in the whisky.

To assemble the cake, slice the sponges horizontally into 5mm (¼in) thick discs. You will only need 3 of the sponges (keep the remaining sponge for another recipe). Fit a layer of sponge in the bottom of a 22cm (8½in) diameter deep loose-bottomed cake tin. Drizzle over one-third of the whisky syrup, then sprinkle over a little coconut. Spread half of the dark chocolate cream on top. Add a second layer of sponge, drizzle with another third of the syrup and sprinkle with coconut. Spread over all the white chocolate cream. Top with the third sponge, drizzle with the remaining syrup and sprinkle over more coconut. Spread over the remaining dark chocolate cream right to the top of the tin and smooth using a palette knife, then sprinkle coconut over the top. Leave to set in the refrigerator overnight.

One hour before serving, remove the cake from the refrigerator and remove the tin using a kitchen blowtorch or the heat of your hands. Dust with icing sugar before serving.

Double-baked chocolate meringue brownie

This is an incredible recipe! The texture of the two contrasting layers, one gooey and rich and the other crunchy with a marshmallow centre, makes this recipe really special.

Serves 8
Preparation time: 25 minutes
Cooking time: 1 hour 10 minutes

For the brownie
250g (8oz) unsalted butter, plus extra for greasing
350g (11½oz) dark chocolate, roughly chopped
300g (10oz) light muscovado sugar
5 large eggs, separated

For the chocolate meringue
4 egg whites
225g (7½oz) golden caster sugar
2 tsp vanilla extract
1 tsp cornflour
50g (2oz) pure cocoa powder

Preheat the oven to 180°C (fan 160°C)/350°F/gas mark 4. Grease a 22cm (8½in) diameter springform cake tin and line with baking paper, making sure it is at least 5cm (2in) above the rim of the tin.

To make the brownie, melt the butter and chocolate together in a heatproof bowl set over a saucepan of barely simmering water, making sure the surface of the water does not touch the bowl. Add the sugar, stirring until it has completely dissolved. Remove from the heat and add the egg yolks.

In a clean, dry bowl, whisk the egg whites to soft peaks. Fold a couple of tablespoons of the egg whites into the chocolate mixture, then fold in the remaining whites using a rubber spatula. Spoon the mixture into the prepared tin and bake in the oven for 40 minutes.

Meanwhile, make the meringue. In a large, clean, dry bowl, whisk the egg whites to stiff peaks, adding the sugar a little at a time, then add the vanilla extract. Sift the cornflour and cocoa powder together, then fold into the meringue until the mixture is even and glossy.

Remove the chocolate brownie from the oven and cover the top with the meringue. Return to the oven for a further 25 minutes, or until the meringue puffs up and a crust forms on the top but the centre is still soft. Leave to cool in the tin. The centre will collapse slightly. Serve warm with crème fraîche or vanilla ice cream.

Chocolate and chestnut truffle cakes

One of my favourite areas of France is Lozère, a mountain region with a great food legacy. Chestnuts are very popular in both cooking and baking, and are used to make chestnut flour, which is gluten free. The flavour of chestnuts works very well with chocolate.

Serves 6
Preparation time: 15 minutes
Cooking time: 25 minutes

125g (4oz) dark chocolate, roughly chopped

125g (4oz) unsalted butter, plus extra for greasing

300g (10oz) sweetened chestnut paste

1 tsp vanilla paste or extract

2 tbsp chestnut flour

4 eggs, separated

chopped glacé chestnuts, to decorate

Preheat the oven to 180°C (fan 160°C)/350°F/gas mark 4. Grease 6 x individual 10cm (4in) diameter loose-bottomed tart tins and line the bases with baking paper.

Gently melt the chocolate and butter together in a heatproof bowl set over a saucepan of barely simmering water, making sure the surface of the water does not touch the bowl.

Remove from the heat and stir in the chestnut paste and vanilla. Add the flour, then beat in the egg yolks one at a time. In a clean, dry bowl, whisk the egg whites to soft peaks, then fold into the chestnut mixture.

Divide the mixture between the prepared tins, filling them three-quarters full. Bake in the oven for 18–20 minutes, or until a skewer inserted into the centres comes out clean. Leave to cool in the tins for 5 minutes, then remove and transfer on to serving plates. Serve warm, topped with glacé chestnuts to decorate, drizzle with honey, along with a jug of pouring cream.

Tip

Sweetened chestnut paste or spread (crème de marrons) is available canned from good delicatessens and some larger supermarkets.

Chocolate omelette soufflé

Not far from where I grew up in France there is a restaurant, at Mont Saint-Michel, famous for its sweet omelette soufflé. This is my take on Madame Poulard's secret recipe.

Serves 1
Preparation time: 10 minutes
Cooking time: 10 minutes

200g (7oz) fresh mixed red berries
2 tsp berry preserve
25g (1oz) dark chocolate, roughly chopped
1 egg yolk
1½ tbsp golden caster sugar, plus an extra 2 tsp
1 tsp vanilla paste or extract
2 egg whites
10g (½oz) unsalted butter
icing sugar, for dusting

Put the berries and berry preserve into a saucepan and cook over a medium heat for 1 minute, or until the berries start to puff up. Remove from the heat and put to one side.

Melt the chocolate in a heatproof bowl set over a saucepan of barely simmering water, making sure the surface of the water does not touch the bowl.

Put the egg yolk, the 2 teaspoons of caster sugar and vanilla into a bowl and mix together, then stir in the chocolate.

In a clean, dry bowl, whisk the egg whites to stiff peaks, adding the remaining caster sugar a little at a time. Fold one-quarter of the egg whites into the chocolate to loosen the mixture, then fold in the remaining whites.

Melt the butter in a small 16cm (6½in) diameter flameproof nonstick frying pan over a medium heat, and meanwhile preheat the grill to a medium-high heat. Spoon the chocolate mixture into the pan, making sure it is an even layer, and cook for 2–3 minutes, then place under the grill for 1 minute, or until set, making sure it does not burn.

Spoon the berry mixture over one half of the omelette. Fold the omelette over to enclose the filling, then dust with icing sugar. Serve immediately.

Tip

Use egg whites at room temperature to get the most volume when whisking.

White chocolate and passion fruit cheesecake

I am a big fan of the baked cheesecake and this recipe is smooth and zesty with a touch of the exotic. It's perfectly sweetened with the white chocolate – a great summer dessert.

Serves 6

Preparation time: 30 minutes, plus cooling and chilling overnight

Cooking time: 1 hour 5 minutes– 1 hour 15 minutes

100g (3½oz) digestive biscuits, crushed

50g (2oz) unsalted butter, melted, plus extra for greasing

125g (4oz) white chocolate, chopped

125ml (4fl oz) single cream

225g (7½oz) cream cheese, softened

225g (7½oz) mascarpone cheese

4 tbsp golden caster sugar

2 tsp vanilla extract

4 eggs, separated

125ml (4fl oz) passion fruit pulp, sieved to remove the pips

passion fruit, to decorate

Preheat the oven to 180°C (fan 160°C)/350°F/gas mark 4. Grease a 20cm (8in) diameter springform cake tin.

Put the crushed biscuits and melted butter into a bowl and mix well. Tip the mixture into the prepared tin and press down with the back of a spoon. Bake in the oven for 10 minutes, or until golden. Leave to cool. Reduce the oven temperature to 150°C (fan 130°C)/300°F/gas mark 2.

Put the chocolate into a heatproof bowl. Put the cream into a small saucepan and heat until steaming hot, but do not let it boil. Pour the cream on to the chocolate and stir until smooth. Put to one side.

In a separate bowl, beat the cream cheese and mascarpone together until smooth. Add the sugar, vanilla and egg yolks. Stir in the white chocolate mixture and passion fruit pulp.

In a large, clean, dry bowl, whisk 2 egg whites to soft peaks (save the remaining 2 egg whites for another recipe). Fold a large spoonful of the egg whites into the batter very vigorously, then gently fold in the remaining whites until smooth.

Spoon the mixture on to the cooled base and bake for 50–60 minutes, or until set but with a slight wobble in the centre. Turn off the oven and leave the cheesecake to cool inside for 2 hours, with the door ajar. Chill in the refrigerator overnight.

Remove from the tin and decorate with fresh passion fruit quarters.

Chocolate coffee baked cheesecake

Cheesecakes are always popular and I have to say I am a great fan of a baked cheesecake. The chocolate in this recipe is enhanced by the addition of the rich, strong coffee flavour.

Serves 6–8

Preparation time: 30 minutes, plus chilling and cooling

Cooking time: 1 hour 35 minutes

175g (6oz) chocolate cookies, crushed

50g (2oz) unsalted butter, melted, plus extra for greasing

250g (8oz) cream cheese

250g (8oz) mascarpone cheese

100g (3½oz) golden caster sugar

150ml (¼ pint) double cream

1 tsp vanilla paste or extract

1 tbsp plain flour

2 eggs, plus 1 egg yolk

1 tsp instant coffee

2 tsp hot water

2 tsp coffee extract

pure cocoa powder, for dusting

For the chocolate topping

15g (½oz) unsalted butter

1 tbsp crème fraîche

50g (2oz) light muscovado sugar

150g (5oz) dark chocolate, finely chopped

1 tsp coffee extract

Preheat the oven to 150°C (fan 130°C)/300°F/gas mark 2. Grease a 22cm (8½in) diameter springform cake tin.

Put the crushed cookies and melted butter into a bowl and mix well. Tip the mixture into the prepared tin and press down with the back of a spoon. Leave to set in the refrigerator for 15 minutes.

Put the cream cheese, mascarpone, sugar, cream, vanilla and flour into a large bowl and beat together until nice and smooth. Beat in the eggs and egg yolk. Dissolve the coffee in the hot water, then beat into the mixture with the coffee extract.

Spoon the mixture on to the chilled base and bake in the oven for 1 hour 30 minutes, or until set but still with a slight wobble in the centre. Turn off the oven and leave the cheesecake to cool inside for 2 hours, with the door ajar. Chill in the refrigerator.

To make the chocolate topping, put the butter, crème fraîche and sugar into a small saucepan and heat gently until melted. Add the chocolate and coffee extract and heat gently for a further 2 minutes, stirring continuously. Remove from the heat, then give the mixture a good whisk. Leave to cool for a few minutes, then pour over the chilled cheesecake. Return to the refrigerator and leave to set.

Remove from the tin and dust generously with cocoa powder. Serve with whipped vanilla cream.

Proper Black Forest gateau

This cake has got a bit of a kitsch reputation, but when done properly it is extremely delicious and light, and will take you on a trip down memory lane.

Serves 10

Preparation time: 45 minutes, plus cooling

Cooking time: 30–35 minutes

6 eggs

1 tsp vanilla extract

250g (8oz) golden caster sugar

50g (2oz) cocoa powder

100g (3½oz) plain flour

150g (5oz) unsalted butter, melted and cooled, plus extra for greasing

150g (5oz) block of dark chocolate

3 tbsp raspberry preserve

40 black cherries, pitted (or canned cherries, drained)

icing sugar, for dusting

For the syrup

200ml (7fl oz) water

175g (6oz) golden caster sugar

2 tbsp kirsch

For the kirsch cream

750ml (1¼ pints) whipping cream

75g (3oz) golden caster sugar

2 tsp vanilla extract

3 tbsp kirsch

First make the sponge. Preheat the oven to 180°C (fan 160°C)/350°F/gas mark 4. Grease 3 x 22cm (8½in) diameter sandwich cake tins and line the bases with baking paper.

In a large bowl, whisk the eggs, vanilla and sugar together using an electric hand whisk until thick and the whisk leaves a trail when lifted above the mixture. Sift the cocoa powder and flour together, then fold in. Stir in the melted butter.

Divide the cake mixture between the prepared tins and bake in the oven for 20–25 minutes, or until springy to the touch. Leave to cool in the tins for 5 minutes, then turn out on to a cooling rack to cool completely.

Meanwhile, shave the block of chocolate either by using a potato peeler or by carefully scraping the blade of a large kitchen knife across the surface of the chocolate. Leave the chocolate shavings in the refrigerator until needed.

To make the syrup, put the water and sugar in a saucepan and bring to the boil, then boil for 5 minutes. Leave to cool, then add the kirsch.

To make the kirsch cream, whip the cream and sugar to firm peaks, then fold in the vanilla and kirsch.

To assemble the cake, level the tops of the sponges, if necessary, using a sharp knife. Place a little kirsch cream on a serving plate and secure one of the sponges on top. Brush the sponge with some of the syrup, then spread over the raspberry preserve. Sandwich together with a second sponge and brush again with the syrup. Spread over a thick layer of the kirsch cream, about 1cm (½in) deep. Cover with the cherries, reserving 8 for decoration. Spread a little more cream over the cherries to secure them, then top with the final sponge, upside down to give an even, flat surface. Brush with the remaining syrup.

Spoon 5 tablespoons of the kirsch cream into a piping bag fitted with a large star nozzle and set aside. Using a palette knife, cover the top and side of the cake with the remaining cream. Carefully stick the chocolate shavings all over the side of the cake with the palm of your hand. Pipe around the edge of the cake and 8 swirls in the middle, then place the reserved cherries on top of the swirls. Serve dusted with icing sugar.

Iced berries with white chocolate sauce

Inspired by a birthday meal at The Ivy restaurant in London, this is a really delicious last-minute solution and a refreshing summer dessert.

Serves 6

Preparation time: 10 minutes, plus chilling

Cooking time: 5 minutes

500g (1lb) mixed frozen berries
150ml (¼ pint) double cream
150g (5oz) white chocolate, roughly chopped
1 tsp vanilla extract
2 tbsp white rum (optional)

Put the frozen berries into the refrigerator 1 hour before serving so that they soften but are still icy.

To make the sauce, put the cream, chocolate and vanilla into a small saucepan and heat gently, stirring continuously, until the chocolate has melted. Leave to cool for 2 minutes, then stir in the rum, if using.

Divide the berries between 6 shallow bowls and pour over the hot sauce. Serve immediately before the fruits completely defrost.

Tip

Use a mixture of blackberries, blueberries, raspberries and redcurrants for a perfect summer dessert.

French bistro chocolate mousse

One of my favourite bistros in Paris is called Chez Janou. Apart from the great atmosphere, the best thing there is the chocolate mousse made the old-fashioned way and served in a large pottery vat with a ladle – and you can eat as much as you want. A dream!

Serves 6
Preparation time: 15 minutes, plus chilling
Cooking time: 5 minutes

250g (8oz) dark chocolate, roughly chopped
65g (2½oz) unsalted butter
6 eggs, separated
pinch of salt

Melt the chocolate and butter together in a heatproof bowl set over a saucepan of barely simmering water, making sure the surface of the water does not touch the bowl. Remove from the heat, then beat in the egg yolks.

In a large, clean, dry bowl, whisk the egg whites and salt to stiff peaks. Fold a large spoonful of the egg whites into the chocolate mixture to loosen, then gently fold in the remaining whites.

Pour the mixture into a serving dish, cover with clingfilm and chill in the refrigerator for at least 4 hours. The mousse is lovely served with Breton Shortbread with Chocolate (see page 56).

Tip

For a grown-up version, add a little orange liqueur, amaretto liqueur or Cognac to the mixture.

Chocolate 'samosas'

Theses unusually sweet samosas are great for a party to serve as a canapé, or even as a dessert with some exotic ice cream, such as mango ice cream.

Makes 4
Preparation time: 10 minutes
Cooking time: 10 minutes

25g (1oz) unsalted butter
2 ripe bananas, sliced
1 tbsp light muscovado sugar
2 sheets of brik or filo pastry
50g (2oz) dark chocolate, finely grated
½ tsp ground cinnamon

Melt half the butter in a frying pan, add the banana slices and sugar and fry for about 4–5 minutes, or until the bananas have caramelized, turning them over halfway during cooking.

Cut the pastry sheets in half. Place banana slices and a good sprinkling of chocolate and cinnamon towards one end of each pastry sheet, then fold up to resemble a triangular 'samosa' shape.

Heat the remaining butter in the frying pan over a medium heat, add the pastries and cook for about 2 minutes each side, or until golden brown all over. Serve immediately.

Chocolate and framboise roulade

This recipe is inspired by my mentors Albert and Michel Roux's classic recipe Le Roule Marquis, which I used to bake when working for them. This easy-to-make recipe is very light and contains no flour, making it a perfect dessert for a casual lunch or dinner.

Serves 10

Preparation time: 35 minutes, plus cooling and chilling

Cooking time: 25 minutes

50g caster sugar

50ml (2fl oz) water

25ml (1fl oz) crème de framboise

300ml (10fl oz) double cream

50g (2oz) icing sugar

500g (1lb) fresh raspberries, plus extra to decorate

For the sponge

butter, for greasing

175g (6oz) dark chocolate, roughly chopped

6 eggs, separated

175g (6oz) caster sugar

1 tsp vanilla paste

2 tbsp cocoa powder, sifted

First make the sponge. Preheat the oven to 180°C (fan 160°C)/350°F/ gas mark 4. Lightly grease a 38cm x 28cm (15 x 11in) baking tray and line with baking paper.

Melt the chocolate in a heatproof bowl set over a saucepan of barely simmering water, making sure the surface of the water does not touch the bowl. Leave to cool for a few minutes.

In a large bowl, whisk the sugar and egg yolks together using an electric hand whisk until pale and creamy. Add the vanilla paste and cooled chocolate and stir until smooth. In a large, clean, dry bowl, whisk the egg whites to stiff peaks. Stir a large spoonful of the egg whites into the chocolate mixture, mixing gently, then fold in the remaining whites. Fold in the cocoa powder.

Spoon the mixture into the prepared tray and gently level the top using a palette knife. Bake in the oven for 18–20 minutes, or until firm to the touch. Place a sheet of nonstick baking paper on top of the sponge, then put a clean, damp tea towel on top of the paper. Leave to cool completely.

Meanwhile, make a syrup by putting the caster sugar and water into a small saucepan and heating gently until the sugar has dissolved. Boil for 2 minutes, then turn off the heat and leave to cool completely before stirring in the framboise.

To assemble the roulade, whip the cream until it just holds its shape. Dust a large piece of nonstick baking paper with some of the icing sugar, then turn the roulade out on to it and peel off the lining paper. Brush the framboise syrup over the cooled sponge, then spread over the whipped cream and cover with the raspberries, pushing them into the cream slightly.

Starting from a long edge, roll up the sponge like a Swiss roll. Roll tightly to start with and use the paper to help you roll it up. The roulade may crack when you do this, but that's part of its charm! Chill in the refrigerator for at least 4 hours.

To serve, trim the ends of the roulade and place on a long serving plate. Dust generously with the remaining icing sugar and serve with extra raspberries. I like to serve this light dessert with a raspberry coulis.

Chocolate 'cassis' royale

This recipe is really worth the effort and is the perfect dessert for a special occasion or get-together, plus it's one of my favourite combinations.

Serves 8

Preparation time: 40 minutes, plus cooling and chilling overnight

Cooking time: 40–45 minutes

butter, for greasing

200g (7oz) dark chocolate, roughly chopped

3 eggs, plus 2 egg yolks

1 tsp cornflour

3 egg whites

300g (10oz) golden caster sugar

300ml (½ pint) balsamic vinegar

300g (10oz) fresh blackcurrants, or frozen and defrosted

For the chocolate mousse

250g (8oz) dark chocolate, roughly chopped

5 egg whites

pinch of salt

For the glaze

200g (7oz) dark chocolate, chopped

200g (7oz) white chocolate, chopped

125ml (4fl oz) milk

75ml (3fl oz) single cream

50g (2oz) golden caster sugar

65g (2½oz) glucose syrup

First make the sponge. Preheat the oven to 180°C (fan 160°C)/350°F/gas mark 4. Grease 2 x 20cm (8in) diameter sandwich cake tins and line with baking paper.

Melt the chocolate in a heatproof bowl set over a saucepan of barely simmering water, making sure the surface of the water does not touch the bowl. Stir the whole eggs and egg yolks together in a bowl, then whisk into the melted chocolate with the cornflour. In a clean, dry bowl, whisk the egg whites to soft peaks. Fold a large spoonful of the egg whites into the chocolate mixture to loosen, then gently fold in the remaining whites.

Divide the mixture between the prepared tins and bake in the oven for 20–25 minutes, or until a skewer inserted into the centres comes out clean. Leave to cool in the tins for 5 minutes before turning out on to a cooling rack to cool completely.

Meanwhile, make a syrup. Put the sugar and vinegar into a saucepan and bring to the boil, then simmer until it forms a thick syrup – almost a caramel. Remove from the heat and put to one side.

To make the chocolate mousse, melt the chocolate as above. In a large, clean, dry bowl, whisk the egg whites and salt to stiff peaks. Fold a good spoonful of the egg whites into the melted chocolate to loosen, then gently fold in the remaining whites.

To assemble the cake, slice the sponges in half horizontally. You will only need 3 of the sponge layers (keep the remaining layer for another recipe). Fit a layer of sponge in the bottom of a 20cm (8in) diameter, loose-bottomed deep cake tin. Cover with the blackcurrants. Reheat the syrup and drizzle all over the fruits, covering them completely. Add a second layer of sponge on top and press down. Spread over the chocolate mousse, leaving enough space for the third sponge on top. If there is any chocolate mousse left, spread this over the top of the sponge using a palette knife. Leave to set in the refrigerator overnight.

When you are ready to serve, make the glaze. Put the dark and white chocolates into separate heatproof bowls. Put the milk, cream, sugar and glucose in a saucepan and bring to the boil. Remove from the heat and pour half over each bowl of chocolate, stirring until it has completely melted.

Remove the cake from the refrigerator and remove from the tin using a kitchen blowtorch or the heat of your hands, then place it on a cooling rack set over a large plate or baking tray. Pour the chocolate glazes on top, letting them drip down the side to cover it completely. Use a palette knife to swirl into a marble effect and smooth evenly, then serve.

Milk, dark and white chocolate verrines

Serving desserts in small shot glasses is now very popular, especially for parties and functions. This trio of chocolate looks great and, of course, tastes great, too.

Serves 8 or fills 20 shot glasses
Preparation time: 35 minutes, plus chilling
Cooking time: 25 minutes

For the dark chocolate layer
75g (3oz) dark chocolate, roughly chopped
1 tbsp golden caster sugar
2 eggs, separated

For the milk chocolate layer
75g (3oz) milk chocolate, roughly chopped
½ tbsp golden caster sugar
2 eggs, separated

For the white chocolate layer
2 egg yolks
2 tsp golden caster sugar
1 tsp cold water
150g (5oz) white chocolate, roughly chopped
250ml (8fl oz) double cream

Start with the dark chocolate layer. Melt the chocolate and sugar together in a heatproof bowl set over a saucepan of barely simmering water, making sure the surface of the water does not touch the bowl. Remove from the heat and stir in the egg yolks. In a clean, dry bowl, whisk the egg whites to firm peaks, then fold into the chocolate mixture. Divide the mixture evenly between glasses or shot glasses. Leave to set in the refrigerator.

Next, make the milk chocolate layer as above. Carefully pour it over the set layer in the glasses and return to the refrigerator to set.

Finally, make the white chocolate layer. Put the egg yolks, sugar and water into a heatproof bowl and mix together. Set the bowl over a saucepan of simmering water and whisk for 10 minutes using an electric hand whisk. Remove from the heat and continue to whisk until the mixture is thick and creamy.

Melt the white chocolate in separate heatproof bowl set over the simmering water, then leave to cool for a few minutes. Lightly whip the cream to soft peaks. Stir the cooled chocolate into the egg mixture, then fold in the whipped cream. Carefully pour the mixture over the set layer in the glasses and chill in the refrigerator for at least 6 hours until completely set. Serve decorated with grated chocolate.

Blackcurrant and vanilla crème brûlée chocolate cake

I love finding surprises when I cut into a cake or dessert. It could be a texture, liquid or, as in this case, a soft and smooth vanilla crème brûlée encased in a blackcurrant-flavoured chocolate mousse.

Serves 8

Preparation time: 50 minutes, plus cooling and freezing overnight

Cooking time: 50 minutes

butter, for greasing

40g (1½oz) golden caster sugar, plus 1 tbsp for sprinkling

2 egg yolks

250ml (8fl oz) double cream

1 vanilla pod, split lengthways

1 x 21cm (8¼in) diameter, 5mm (¼in) deep chocolate sponge cake (use any chocolate sponge recipe)

4 tbsp blackcurrant preserve

For the chocolate mousse

50ml (2fl oz) water

50g (2oz) golden caster sugar

2 blackcurrant tea bags

225g (7½oz) dark chocolate, roughly chopped

400ml (14fl oz) whipping cream

75g (3oz) egg yolks

For the ganache

125ml (4fl oz) double cream

125g (4oz) dark chocolate, chopped

25g (1oz) unsalted butter

Preheat the oven to 110°C (fan 90°C)/225°F/gas mark ¼. Lightly grease a 20cm (8in) diameter ovenproof dish (the dish must be slightly smaller than your cake ring or tin) and sprinkle it with the 1 tablespoon of sugar.

To make the crème brûlée, put the egg yolks and remaining sugar into a heatproof bowl and mix together. Pour the cream into a saucepan, add the vanilla pod and bring to the boil. Remove from the heat and pass the hot cream through a fine sieve on to the egg mixture, stirring continuously. Pour the mixture into the prepared dish and cook in the oven for 30 minutes, or until lightly set. Leave to cool, then freeze for 2 hours.

Meanwhile, make the mousse. Put the water, sugar and tea bags into a saucepan over a high heat and bring to the boil, stirring until the sugar has dissolved. Remove from the heat and leave the syrup to infuse.

Melt the chocolate in a heatproof bowl set over a saucepan of barely simmering water, making sure the surface of the water does not touch the bowl. Leave to cool. Whip the cream to soft peaks. Squeeze the syrup from the tea bags and bring back to the boil. In a large bowl, whisk the egg yolks using an electric hand whisk, then pour in the syrup and continue whisking the mixture until it is light and fluffy. Leave to cool, then stir into the cooled chocolate. Fold in the whipped cream.

To assemble the cake, slice the chocolate sponge in half horizontally and brush each layer with blackcurrant preserve. Place a 22cm (8½in) diameter ring or springform cake tin on a baking sheet and fit a layer of sponge in the bottom, preserve side up. Spread over half of the chocolate mousse.

Turn out the crème brûlée and place on top of the mousse. Spread over the remaining mousse and top with the remaining sponge, preserve side down. Return to the freezer to set for several hours or overnight.

To make the ganache, put the cream into a saucepan and heat gently, then carefully stir in the chocolate until melted and smooth. Remove from the heat. Cut the butter into small pieces and add to the chocolate mixture, stirring continuously until thoroughly incorporated.

Remove the frozen dessert from the ring or tin using a kitchen blowtorch or the heat of your hands and place it on a cooling rack set over a large plate or baking tray. Pour over the warm ganache, smooth with a palette knife and leave it to set. Serve at room temperature.

White chocolate tiramisu

The Italian classic and now international sensation, revisited by me with the addition of exotic cardamom, coffee and white chocolate. This recipe is best made the day before serving.

Serves 6
Preparation time: 25 minutes, plus chilling overnight
Cooking time: 5 minutes

butter, for greasing
25g (1oz) cocoa powder
2 tsp ground cardamom
100ml (3½fl oz) hot black coffee
175g (6oz) white chocolate, roughly chopped
250g (8oz) mascarpone cheese
3 eggs, separated
pinch of salt
13 speculoos biscuits
icing sugar, for dusting

Grease 6 ramekin dishes, then dust with some of the cocoa powder.

Add the cardamom to the hot black coffee and leave to infuse while it cools.

Melt the chocolate in a heatproof bowl set over a saucepan of barely simmering water, making sure the surface of the water does not touch the bowl.

Put the mascarpone in a large bowl and whisk in the egg yolks. Stir in the melted chocolate. In a clean, dry bowl, whisk the egg whites and salt to soft peaks, then gently fold into the mascarpone mixture.

Dunk 6 biscuits into the infused coffee one at a time, and place one in each of the ramekins. Add a layer of the mascarpone mixture. Repeat with another layer of dipped biscuits, then finally top with a layer of mascarpone.

Crumble the remaining biscuit and sprinkle a little on the top of each ramekin. Chill in the refrigerator overnight. Serve dusted with the remaining cocoa powder and some icing sugar.

Tip

Speculoos biscuits are thin, very crunchy biscuits originally from the Netherlands, and are now available in larger supermarkets or specialist food stores.

White chocolate, raspberry and lemon Battenberg

This is my take on a great British cake, making it lighter, colourful and a touch more contemporary in presentation, too.

Serves 8

Preparation time: 45 minutes, plus cooling

Cooking time: 30–35 minutes

350g (11½oz) unsalted butter, softened, plus extra for greasing

350g (11½oz) golden caster sugar

275g (9oz) self-raising flour

100g (3½oz) ground almonds

1 tsp baking powder

6 eggs

1 tsp vanilla paste or extract

2 tbsp milk

2 tbsp freeze-dried raspberry pieces

2 tsp raspberry extract

few drops of pink food colouring

2 tsp lemon extract

few drops of yellow food colouring

150g (5oz) raspberry preserve

icing sugar, for dusting

300g (10oz) white modelling chocolate

fresh raspberries, to decorate

Preheat the oven to 180°C (fan 160°C)/350°F/gas mark 4. Grease 2 x 20cm (8in) square cake tins or a Battenberg tin and line with baking paper.

Put the butter, caster sugar, flour, ground almonds, baking powder, eggs, vanilla and milk into a large bowl and beat together until smooth. Divide the mixture in half and put one half into another bowl. Mix the dried raspberries, raspberry extract and pink food colouring into one batter until a pink colour. Mix the lemon extract and yellow food colouring into the other batter until you get a nice bright yellow colour.

Spoon each mixture into a prepared tin and bake in the oven for 25–30 minutes, or until a skewer inserted into the centres comes out clean. Leave to cool in the tins.

Heat the raspberry preserve in a small saucepan until runny, then pass through a sieve into a bowl. Trim the sponges, each to the same width as the sponge height, to form 4 identical long rectangles, 2 from each colour (freeze any leftover sponge for another time). Using a patterned rolling pin on a work surface lightly dusted with icing sugar, roll out the white modelling chocolate to a rectangle, 25 x 20cm (10 x 8in).

Place a pink and yellow sponge rectangle side by side, brushing some preserve in between them to stick together. Brush some preserve over the top, then place the remaining pink and yellow sponges on top, alternating the colours and sticking together with more preserve. Brush the outside of the sponges with preserve but not the cut ends.

Carefully place the stacked sponge in the centre of the modelling chocolate, then tightly wrap the chocolate around the cake. Turn it over so that it is seam side down and trim off any excess. Dust a few fresh raspberries with icing sugar and arrange on top to decorate.

Tip

If the sponges are baked the day before the cake is assembled, they are less likely to crumble.

Decadent chocolate pavlova

I discovered the pavlova when I arrived in the UK and ever since I have been creating new versions of this versatile, delicious dessert. This is my latest one – a chocolate version, of course!

Serves 10

Preparation time: 25 minutes, plus cooling

Cooking time: 1 hour 45 minutes

6 egg whites

350g (11½oz) golden caster sugar

1 tbsp cornflour

4 tbsp pure cocoa powder

1 tsp white wine vinegar

100g (3½oz) dark chocolate chips

100g (3½oz) white chocolate chips

100g (3½oz) mini marshmallows

500ml (17fl oz) whipping cream

2 tsp vanilla extract

50g (2oz) dark chocolate, finely grated

icing sugar, for dusting

Preheat the oven to 120°C (fan 100°C)/250°F/gas mark ½. Line a large baking sheet with baking paper.

In a large, clean, dry bowl, whisk the egg whites to stiff peaks, adding the sugar a little at a time. Sift the cornflour and cocoa powder together, then gently fold into the egg whites with the vinegar until combined. Fold in the chocolate chips and marshmallows but do not over-mix.

Using a rubber spatula, spread some of the mixture on to the prepared baking sheet to form a 22cm (8½in) diameter disc, then pile high with the remaining mixture.

Bake in the oven for 1 hour 45 minutes, or until crunchy on the outside and gooey in the centre. Leave on the paper and transfer to a cooling rack to cool completely. It will sink and crack a little.

Whip the cream and vanilla together to firm peaks, then pile high on the meringue. Dust with the grated chocolate and icing sugar. Serve immediately.

Tip

Use a baking sheet that is large enough to allow a 22cm (8½in) diameter meringue to expand during cooking.

Chocolate fondants with orange and muscat compote

Sinfully sweet and intensely indulgent, this recipe is a chocoholic's dream!
The orange compote marries the classic chocolate and orange combination.

Serves 4

Preparation time: 15 minutes

Cooking time: 15 minutes

2 tsp cocoa powder

125g (4oz) unsalted butter, plus
extra for greasing

200g (7oz) dark chocolate,
roughly chopped

75g (3oz) golden caster sugar

2 eggs, plus 2 egg yolks

25g (1oz) plain flour

For the orange compote

1 large orange, peeled and
segmented

2 tsp golden caster sugar

1 tsp cornflour

100ml (3½fl oz) muscat wine

Preheat the oven to 180°C (fan 160°C)/350°F/gas
mark 4. Grease 4 x 150ml (¼ pint) individual pudding
moulds, then coat with the cocoa powder, tapping out
any excess. Transfer the moulds to a baking sheet.

Melt the chocolate and butter together in a heatproof
bowl set over a pan of barely simmering water, making
sure the surface of the water does not touch the bowl,
stirring until smooth. Leave to cool for a few minutes.

In a large bowl, whisk the sugar, eggs and egg yolks
together using an electric hand whisk until thick, pale
and fluffy and doubled in volume. Gently stir the cooled
chocolate into the mixture, then fold in the flour.

Divide the mixture between the prepared pudding
moulds, filling them three-quarters full. Cook in the
oven for 12 minutes.

Meanwhile, make the orange compote. Put the orange
segments into a frying pan and heat gently, then stir in
the sugar and cook gently until the mixture starts to
sizzle. Mix the cornflour with a little water to a paste,
then add with the wine to the oranges and cook until
the compote has reduced by half.

Remove the fondants from the oven and use a sharp
knife to slide around the edge of each pudding mould
to release. Invert on to 4 plates and carefully remove the
moulds. Serve immediately with the orange compote.

White chocolate strawberry tarts

I think this recipe shouts of summer – buttery shortcrust pastry, sweet strawberry compote, light and decadent white chocolate Chantilly and flavoursome seasonal strawberries...

Serves 6

Preparation time: 40 minutes, plus chilling and cooling

Cooking time: 10 minutes

For the pastry

300g (10oz) plain flour, plus extra for dusting

4 tbsp golden caster sugar

200g (7oz) unsalted butter, chopped into pieces

2 egg yolks

2 tbsp cold water

2 tsp vanilla paste or extract

For the compote

50g (2oz) golden caster sugar

200g (7oz) strawberries, hulled and finely chopped

1 tsp vanilla extract

For the Chantilly cream

100g (3½oz) white chocolate, roughly chopped

250ml (8fl oz) whipping cream

150g (5oz) strawberries, hulled and halved, for decoration

First make the pastry. Sift the flour into a large mixing bowl and stir in the sugar. Using your fingertips, rub in the butter until the mixture resembles breadcrumbs. Make a well in the centre and add the rest of the ingredients. Again using your fingertips, mix together to make a smooth dough. Turn out on to a floured surface and gather together into a ball. Cover with clingfilm and chill for at least 30 minutes before using.

Lightly grease 6 x 10cm (4in) diameter individual tart tins. Roll out the pastry and use it to line the tins. Prick the base of each pastry case, then chill in the refrigerator for 15 minutes.

Line each pastry case with baking paper and fill with baking beans. Bake in a preheated oven, 180°C (fan 160°C)/350°F/gas mark 4, for 8–10 minutes, or until the cases are just set, then remove the paper and beans and cook empty for a further 4–5 minutes, or until the bases are dry and crisp. Remove from the tins once cool.

To make the compote, put the sugar and chopped strawberries into a saucepan and cook over a medium heat until the fruits turn to a thick compote, then stir in the vanilla. Leave to cool.

To make the Chantilly cream, melt the white chocolate in a heatproof bowl set over a saucepan of barely simmering water, making sure the surface of the water does not touch the bowl. Leave to cool for a few minutes. Meanwhile, whip the cream to soft peaks, then fold one-quarter of the cream into the cooled chocolate. Fold in the remaining cream without over-mixing.

To assemble the tarts, spoon some compote on to the bottom of each tart and spread with the Chantilly cream, then top with the halved strawberries.

Mini chocolate syrup cakes

Theses cute puddings are perfect winter warmers and a great ending to a long, lazy Sunday lunch. The amaretto gives them a delicious continental touch. Best served with a dark chocolate sauce (see page 168).

Serves 6

Preparation time: 25 minutes

Cooking time: 25–30 minutes

100g (3½oz) unsalted butter, plus extra for greasing

100g (3½oz) dark chocolate, roughly chopped

2 eggs

50g (2oz) dark muscovado sugar

40g (1½oz) golden syrup

75g (3oz) ground almonds

15g (½oz) plain flour, plus extra for dusting

½ tsp baking powder

2 tbsp amaretto liqueur

6 amaretti biscuits, plus extra to decorate

Grease 6 x 150ml (¼ pint) individual pudding moulds and dust with flour, tapping out any excess. Cut out 6 small circles of baking paper to fit the bases and drop one into each mould. Grease 6 pieces of foil, each about 15cm (6in) square.

Put the butter and chocolate into a saucepan and heat gently until melted. Leave to cool.

Whisk the eggs, sugar and golden syrup together in a large bowl using an electric hand whisk until thick and foamy. Fold in the cooled chocolate mixture using a rubber spatula. Mix the ground almonds, flour and baking powder together in a separate bowl, then fold into the mixture with 1 tablespoon of the amaretto.

Preheat the oven to 200°C (fan 180°C)/400°F/gas mark 6.

Put the biscuits in a small bowl and splash over the remaining amaretto. Fill the prepared pudding moulds one-third full with cake mixture, then drop a soaked biscuit into each. Top with the remaining mixture, leaving 1cm (½in) between the mixture and the top of the moulds. Loosely scrunch a foil square over the top of each mould.

Put the moulds into a roasting tin and pour in hot water to come about halfway up the sides of the moulds. Bake in the oven for 20–25 minutes, or until a skewer inserted into the centres comes out clean.

To serve the puddings, use a sharp knife to slide around the edge of each pudding mould to release. Invert on to plates and carefully remove the moulds. Spoon over some chocolate sauce, allowing it to drizzle over the edges, then sprinkle with broken amaretti biscuits. Serve immediately.

Old-fashioned dusted truffles

Truffles & Treats

Old-fashioned dusted truffles

I have fond memories of this simple but delicious recipe. As kids we spent hours making truffles for the festive season. By the end we were covered head to toe with cocoa powder, but it was still great fun to make them. These are fresh truffles and need to be kept in the refrigerator and consumed within 1 week – that's if you can resist eating them straight away!

Makes 30

Preparation time: 15 minutes, plus chilling

Cooking time: 5 minutes

250g (8oz) dark chocolate, chopped

2 tbsp milk

1 tbsp espresso coffee

100g (3½oz) unsalted butter, softened

2 egg yolks

25g (1oz) cocoa powder, sifted

Gently melt the chocolate and milk together in a heatproof bowl set over a saucepan of barely simmering water, making sure the surface of the water does not touch the bowl.

Remove from the heat and stir in the coffee, butter and egg yolks until combined. Transfer the mixture to a bowl and leave to set in the refrigerator for 4 hours.

Place the cocoa powder on a plate. Using a dessertspoon, scoop out spoonfuls of the chocolate mixture. Coat your hands in cocoa powder to prevent the mixture from sticking and roll the chocolate mixture between the palms of your hand to form walnut-sized balls.

Using a fork, roll the truffles in the cocoa powder to coat. Store the truffles in an airtight container in the refrigerator for up to 1 week. See previous page for the finished result.

Tip

It is best to remove the truffles from the refrigerator and bring to room temperature before serving.

1. Melt the chocolate and milk together.

2. Off the heat, stir in the coffee, butter and egg yolks, then leave to set.

3. Scoop out spoonfuls of chocolate mixture and roll into balls.

4. Roll the truffles in cocoa powder to coat.

Pink fizz champagne truffles

If like me you like rosé champagne and chocolate, this after-dinner truffle with extra pop will be your new favourite treat.

Makes 15

Preparation time: 15 minutes, plus chilling

Cooking time: 5 minutes

100g (3½oz) dark chocolate, chopped

100ml (3½fl oz) single cream

2 tsp Marc de Champagne

2 tsp plain popping candy

5 tbsp icing sugar

1 tsp pink food colouring

Put the chocolate into a heatproof bowl. Put the cream into a small saucepan and heat until steaming hot, but do not let it boil, then pour on to the chocolate and stir gently until melted, smooth and glossy. Leave to cool.

When cooled, stir in the champagne, then the popping candy. Leave to set in the refrigerator for at least 4 hours.

Put the icing sugar and food colouring into a blender and whizz together. Tip on to a plate.

Using a teaspoon, scoop up the ganache and roll between the palms of your hand to form perfect round shapes. Using a fork, roll the truffles in the pink icing sugar to coat. Store the truffles in an airtight container in the refrigerator for up to 1 week.

Tip

Dust your hands with icing sugar before rolling the truffles to stop the ganache sticking.

Crisp chocolate bonbons

Very crunchy, very nutty and, of course, very chocolaty; theses sweets make a perfect gift wrapped in cellophane wrappers and placed in a beautiful glass jar.

Makes 24

Preparation time: 15 minutes, plus cooling and chilling

Cooking time: 5 minutes

200g (7oz) milk chocolate, roughly chopped

200ml (7fl oz) crème fraîche

50g (2oz) crispy rice cereal

50g (2oz) nibbed almonds, roasted (see Tip on page 44)

50g (2oz) chopped hazelnuts, roasted (see Tip on page 44)

Line a 19cm (7½in) square shallow baking tin with baking paper.

Melt the chocolate in a heatproof bowl set over a saucepan of barely simmering water until smooth and glossy, making sure the surface of the water does not touch the bowl. Meanwhile, put the crème fraîche into a saucepan and heat gently, then stir into the melted chocolate. Leave to cool.

Divide the chocolate mixture between 3 small bowls and stir one of the dry ingredients into each.

Spoon the coated crispy rice cereal into the prepared tin and press down with the back of a spoon. Leave to set in the refrigerator.

Once set, spread the coated almonds over the top, then return to the refrigerator and leave to set.

Repeat with the hazelnut mixture to form 3 layers, then cover with clingfilm and chill in the refrigerator for at least 4 hours until completely set.

Remove from the tin on to a chopping board and cut into 24 small rectangles using a large, sharp knife. Wrap the bonbons in sweet wrapping paper. Store in an airtight container for up to 1 week.

Palet d'or

Palet d'or are a chocolatier classic and most good pâtisseries will have some on display in their stores. They are smooth chocolates, flavoured with coffee and hazelnut and, as the name suggests, decorated with gold leaf.

Makes about 60

Preparation time: 45 minutes, plus standing and chilling

Cooking time: 10 minutes

For the ganache

200g (7oz) dark chocolate, roughly chopped

150ml (¼ pint) double cream

2 tsp coffee extract

12g (½oz) glucose syrup

20g (¾oz) hazelnut spread

20g (¾oz) unsalted butter

1 tsp vanilla paste or extract

For the coating

300g (10oz) dark chocolate, finely chopped

few sheets of edible gold leaf or chocolate transfer acetate sheet with a gold design

To make the ganache, melt the chocolate in a large heatproof bowl set over a saucepan of barely simmering water, making sure the surface of the water does not touch the bowl.

Put the cream into a small saucepan and heat until steaming hot, but do not let it boil. Stir in the coffee extract, then leave to cool for a few minutes. Stir the cooled cream into the melted chocolate until smooth and glossy. Gently stir in the glucose, hazelnut spread, butter and vanilla. Leave to stand for a couple of hours, stirring occasionally to stop the mixture separating.

Line a 20cm (8in) square shallow baking tin with baking paper. Spread the ganache about 1.5cm (¾in) thick in the tin and smooth over the top using a palette knife. Cover with clingfilm and leave to set in the refrigerator for at least 2 hours.

When ready to coat, melt, cool and reheat the dark chocolate following the Tempering technique on page 12. If using, crumble the gold leaf all over a sheet of acetate.

Carefully turn out the ganache on to a chopping board and cut into 2cm (¾in) squares using a large, sharp knife. Using a fork, dip each one into the tempered chocolate to completely coat, tapping off any excess, then carefully place on the prepared acetate sheet. Before the chocolates set completely, cover with another sheet of acetate, smoothing it gently. Leave to set in the refrigerator.

When set, very carefully remove the chocolates from the acetate sheets and place, gold side up, in a beautiful box or on a serving tray. Store in a cool, dry place for up to 1 week.

Chocolate-coated cherries

These delicate cherries soaked in brandy and coated with chocolate are to die for, but they are not for the faint-hearted, as the alcohol contained in them is quite strong!

Makes about 60

Preparation time: 2 hours, plus 2 months marinating, setting and resting

Cooking time: 10 minutes

icing sugar, for dusting

75g (3oz) chocolate vermicelli

300g (10oz) white fondant (available from a cake decorating shop or your local baker)

350g (11½oz) dark chocolate, finely chopped

For the cherries

500g (1lb) fresh cherries with stalks, washed and dried

125g (4oz) golden caster sugar

2 cinnamon sticks

2 tsp vanilla paste or extract

6 coriander seeds, crushed

500ml (17fl oz) Cognac

To marinate the cherries, pack the fruit nice and tightly into a sterilized preserving jar (see Tip on page 164), alternating each layer of fruit with a sprinkle of sugar. Push in the cinnamon sticks, vanilla and coriander. Cover completely with the brandy right to the top of the jar and seal. Leave to soak for 2 months in a dark, cool, dry place. Gently shake the jar every 2–3 weeks to make sure the sugar dissolves.

Carefully drain the cherries, reserving the brandy for later use, and pat dry with kitchen paper. Line a baking sheet with baking paper and dust generously with icing sugar. Place the chocolate vermicelli in a shallow bowl.

Melt the fondant in a small saucepan until liquid and hot (50°C/122°F on a sugar thermometer, if you have one). Dip the cherries into the fondant using the stalks and place on the prepared sheet. Leave to cool and set.

Melt, cool and reheat the chocolate following the Tempering technique on page 12.

Using the stalks, dip each cherry into the tempered chocolate, making sure that a quarter of the stalk is coated to seal the fruit completely. Carefully shake off any excess chocolate. Dip the bases into the vermicelli before placing on a sheet of baking paper. Leave to set, then put into a sterilized airtight container. Leave for 1 week in a cool, dry place before eating – by that time the fondant will have melted and transformed into alcoholic syrup.

Tip

The white fondant must still be white when it has melted – if it is clear, it is too hot and needs to cool before use.

Large hazelnut bouchées

Bouchées are large chocolate treats, which you usually graze on throughout the day, making the indulgent pleasure last even longer.

Makes 36
Preparation time: 30 minutes, plus cooling, chilling and setting
Cooking time: 20 minutes

For the filling
150g (5oz) hazelnuts
125g (4oz) golden caster sugar
butter, for greasing
75g (3oz) milk chocolate, roughly chopped
25g (1oz) dark chocolate, roughly chopped

For the coating
100g (3½oz) dark chocolate, roughly chopped
100g (3½oz) milk chocolate, roughly chopped
25g (1oz) nibbed almonds, roasted (see Tip on page 44)
a couple of pinches of coarse sea salt crystals

First make the filling. Preheat the oven to 180°C (fan 160°C)/350°F/gas mark 4. Place the hazelnuts on a baking sheet and roast in the oven for 10 minutes until lightly golden.

Meanwhile, put the sugar into a heavy-based saucepan and heat until it forms a dark caramel, then stir in the roasted hazelnuts and turn on to a greased baking sheet. Leave to cool completely.

When cool, break the brittle into smaller pieces and place in a blender, then whizz to a fine powder.

Melt the milk chocolate and dark chocolate together in a heatproof bowl set over a saucepan of barely simmering water, making sure the surface of the water does not touch the bowl. Remove from the heat and stir in the hazelnut powder, mixing to a smooth, thick paste.

Using a teaspoon, fill a silicone round-shaped chocolate mould with the mixture and leave to set in the refrigerator. When completely set, carefully remove the chocolates from the moulds. (The filling makes about 36 chocolates, so you may have to make these in batches.)

To coat the bouchées, melt both chocolates together in a heatproof bowl as above, then remove from the heat and stir in the almonds and salt. Using a fork, dip the chocolate balls into the melted chocolate to coat completely, tapping off any excess. Place on a sheet of baking paper or acetate and leave to set. Store in an airtight container for up to 1 week.

Honey and milk chocolate bars

Kids are usually fonder of milk and white chocolate so what could be more fun than making your own treats before eating them? This easy-to-make recipe will be a hit with adults, too.

Serves 8

Preparation time: 10 minutes, plus chilling

Cooking time: 10 minutes

200g (7oz) milk chocolate, roughly chopped, plus an extra 25g (1oz) for the topping

40g (1½oz) unsalted butter, plus extra for greasing

2 tbsp clear honey

2 tbsp condensed milk

75g (3oz) crispy rice cereal

25g (1oz) desiccated coconut

150g (5oz) white chocolate, roughly chopped

Grease an 18cm (7in) square shallow baking tin and line with baking paper.

Put the milk chocolate, butter, honey and condensed milk into a small saucepan and heat gently until melted and smooth, then stir in the crispy rice cereal and coconut.

Spoon the mixture into the prepared tin and level the top with the back of a spoon. Leave to set in the refrigerator for at least 30 minutes.

Melt the white chocolate in a heatproof bowl set over a saucepan of barely simmering water, making sure the surface of the water does not touch the bowl. Leave to cool for a few minutes, then spread over the top of the rice cake. Return to the refrigerator to set.

Melt the remaining 25g (1oz) of milk chocolate as above, then spoon the chocolate into a small piping bag with a small hole snipped at the tip. Drizzle a pattern over the white chocolate and leave to set at room temperature.

Remove from the tin on to a chopping board and cut into rectangular bars using a large, sharp knife. Store in an airtight container or wrap in cellophane bags for gifts.

Tip

This is an easy recipe for kids to make but will require adult supervision and help, especially when cutting the fridge cake into bars with the sharp knife!

Mint chocolate squares

After-dinner mints have always been the perfect way to finish a meal when served with strong coffee or infusions. These little square ones will become a favourite.

Makes 36

Preparation time: 10 minutes, plus chilling

Cooking time: 10 minutes

butter, for greasing

375g (12oz) dark chocolate, roughly chopped

325g (11oz) icing sugar

1 tbsp vegetable oil

2 tbsp milk

¼ tsp peppermint extract

Grease a 20cm (8in) square, 6cm (2½in) deep baking tin. Line the base and sides with baking paper, allowing it to hang over the sides.

Melt the chocolate in a heatproof bowl set over a saucepan of barely simmering water, making sure the surface of the water does not touch the bowl. Spread half of the melted chocolate over the base of the prepared tin and smooth using a small palette knife. Chill for 15 minutes, or until set.

Sift the icing sugar into a heatproof bowl, then stir in the oil and milk to form a thick paste. Place the bowl over a saucepan of simmering water and heat for a few minutes, stirring. Stir in the peppermint, then leave to cool for 2 minutes.

Pour the peppermint mixture over the chocolate in the tin, spreading with a spatula. Return to the refrigerator for 15 minutes, or until just set.

Cover the peppermint layer with the remaining melted chocolate, then make a wave pattern on the top using a fork. Chill in the refrigerator for at least 1 hour.

Carefully lift out of the tin on to a chopping board and cut into 36 small squares using a large, warm knife. Store in an airtight container for up to 1 week.

Tip

If the peppermint mixture is too thick once cooled for 2 minutes, add an extra 1 teaspoon of milk at a time to loosen.

Lapsang souchong pralines

Chocolate works with so many flavours and that's why chocolatiers are having a ball creating confections using extraordinary scents. The smoky flavour of the lapsang souchong tea is a perfect example.

Makes 24

Preparation time: 15 minutes, plus cooling and chilling

Cooking time: 10 minutes

150g (5oz) dark chocolate, roughly chopped

150ml (¼ pint) double cream

2 tbsp loose leaf lapsang souchong tea

25g (1oz) dark muscovado sugar

2 tsp vanilla paste or extract

15g (½oz) cocoa powder

Melt the chocolate in a heatproof bowl set over a saucepan of barely simmering water, making sure the surface of the water does not touch the bowl. Remove from the heat.

Put the cream, tea and sugar into a small saucepan and bring to a gentle simmer over a low heat. Leave to cool and infuse for 4–5 minutes.

Pass the infused cream through a fine sieve into a bowl. Stir in the vanilla, then pour over the melted chocolate and stir until smooth and glossy. Leave to cool and set to a piping consistency.

Line a baking sheet with baking paper. Spoon the mixture into a piping bag fitted with a 2cm (¾in) diameter plain piping nozzle, then pipe long lengths on to the prepared baking sheet. Leave to set in the refrigerator.

When solid, cut the lengths into 5cm (2in) oblong sticks using a sharp knife. Sift the cocoa powder into a shallow bowl, then roll the sticks in the cocoa to coat. Place on a serving plate or in a gift box.

Chocolate guimauve

Marshmallows have made a huge comeback and are no longer just for kids. Gourmet mallows are everywhere and these chocolate ones are definitely for grown-ups.

Makes 45 squares

Preparation time: 25 minutes, plus chilling

Cooking time: 10 minutes

50g (2oz) cocoa powder
150ml (¼ pint) water
2 tsp amaretto liqueur
200g (7oz) golden caster sugar
2 tbsp gelatine powder
2 tsp vanilla paste
125ml (4fl oz) corn syrup
125g (4oz) dark chocolate, roughly chopped

Line a 20cm (8in) square, 6cm (2½in) deep baking tin with baking paper, then dust generously with some of the cocoa powder.

Put the water, amaretto, sugar and gelatine powder into a small saucepan over a low heat and stir until it has dissolved but do not let it boil. Remove from the heat and stir in the vanilla paste.

Transfer the mixture to the bowl of a free-standing mixer, add the corn syrup and whisk to stiff peaks – this may take up to 12 minutes.

Meanwhile, melt the chocolate in a heatproof bowl set over a saucepan of barely simmering water, making sure the surface of the water does not touch the bowl. Leave to cool for a few minutes, then fold into the whisked mallow.

Pour the mixture into the prepared tin and spread level using a damp palette knife. Leave to set in the refrigerator for at least 1 hour.

Dust a chopping board with some more of the cocoa powder and sift the remaining cocoa powder into a shallow bowl. Turn out the mallow on to the board, then cut into bite-sized cubes. Using a fork, roll the mallows in the sifted cocoa powder, shaking off the excess. Store in an airtight container for up to 2 weeks.

Chocolate honeycomb

I love offering these rough shards of sweet honeycomb as gifts wrapped up in cellophane. They are great to eat on their own or to crumble on ice cream.

Makes 1 x 20cm (8in) square
Preparation time: 10 minutes, plus setting
Cooking time: 8 minutes

unsalted butter, for greasing
200g (7oz) golden caster sugar
4 tbsp golden syrup
25g (1oz) dark chocolate, finely chopped
1 tbsp bicarbonate of soda

Grease a 20cm (8in) square shallow baking tin.

Melt the sugar and golden syrup together in a heavy-based saucepan over a low heat, then increase the heat to medium and simmer for 3–4 minutes, or until the mixture is thick and a dark caramel colour.

Remove from the heat, add the chocolate and immediately whisk in the bicarbonate of soda so that the mixture froths up – stand back just in case.

Pour the mixture into the prepared tin and leave to set at room temperature for about 2–3 hours.

Remove from the tin and break into large pieces using a rolling pin. Store in cellophane bags for up to 1 week.

Tip

To make the honeycomb more luxurious, drizzle some melted white and milk chocolate on the top of the pieces before serving or wrapping them.

Chocolate fudge

I had never come across fudge before I arrived in the UK, but it didn't take me long to become fond of these sweets eaten mostly on trips to seaside towns. They make such a great gift when beautifully wrapped.

Makes 36

Preparation time: 10 minutes, plus chilling

Cooking time: 5 minutes

400g (13oz) dark chocolate, roughly chopped

400ml can condensed milk

25g (1oz) unsalted butter, plus extra for greasing

100g (3½oz) golden icing sugar

Lightly grease a 19cm (7½in) square shallow baking tin.

Put the chocolate, condensed milk and butter into a small saucepan and melt gently over a low heat, stirring occasionally, until smooth and silky. Sift in the icing sugar and mix thoroughly.

Press the mixture into the prepared tin and smooth over the top with the back of a spoon. Cover with clingfilm and leave to set in the refrigerator for 1 hour.

Turn out the fudge on to a chopping board and cut into 36 squares. Store in an airtight container in a cool, dry place for up to 1 week.

Tip

For variety, try adding chopped nuts or dried fruits to the mixture.

Chocolate orange truffles

When you hear about the popular combination of chocolate and orange you always think dark chocolate, but it does work surprisingly well with white chocolate too, if not better.

Makes 24

Preparation time: 40 minutes, plus chilling and setting

Cooking time: 8 minutes

75ml (3fl oz) double cream

500g (1lb) white chocolate, chopped

25g (1oz) unsalted butter

4 tsp orange liqueur

50g (2oz) candied orange peel, finely chopped

50g (2oz) dark chocolate, roughly chopped

Put the cream into a small saucepan and heat to just below boiling point. Stir in half of the white chocolate and the butter until smooth. Add the liqueur and orange peel, then transfer the mixture to a bowl and leave to firm up in the refrigerator.

Line a baking sheet with baking paper. Using a teaspoon, scoop up small amounts of the ganache, shape into balls with your hands and place on the baking sheet.

Melt the remaining white chocolate in a heatproof bowl set over a saucepan of barely simmering water, making sure the surface of the water does not touch the bowl. Leave to cool for a few minutes.

Using a fork, dip each ganache ball into the melted white chocolate, then return to the lined baking sheet and leave to set.

Melt the dark chocolate as above and leave to cool for a few minutes. Spoon the melted dark chocolate into a small piping bag fitted with a very thin piping nozzle, then pipe fine lines on to each truffle and leave to set. Store the truffles in an airtight container in a cool, dry place for up to 1 week.

Tip

If the balls of ganache soften before you are ready to dip them in the melted white chocolate, place them in the refrigerator to firm up, or place them in the freezer for 10 minutes.

Soft chocolate butter toffee

Brittany, where I grew up, is the only region of France that uses salted butter for everyday use. Toffee is one of those sweets that work so well with a little bit of salt added, too.

Makes 25

Preparation time: 20 minutes, plus setting overnight

Cooking time: 20 minutes

oil, for greasing

50g (2oz) dark chocolate, 99% cocoa solids or the darkest you can get, roughly chopped

4 tsp water

100g (3½oz) glucose syrup

250g (8oz) golden caster sugar

100g (3½oz) salted butter

200ml (7fl oz) double cream

Lightly oil a 20cm (8in) square shallow baking tin.

Melt the chocolate in a heatproof bowl set over a saucepan of barely simmering water, making sure the surface of the water does not touch the bowl.

Meanwhile, place the water, glucose and sugar in a heavy-based saucepan and heat over a medium heat until it forms a nice blond caramel. Remove from the heat and add 15g (½oz) of the butter to cool the mixture.

Put the cream into a small saucepan and heat slightly, then slowly pour it into the caramel, stirring gently. Add the remaining butter, return the pan to the heat and heat until the mixture reaches 118°C (244°F) on a sugar thermometer.

Remove from the heat and stir in the melted chocolate until smooth. Pour into the prepared tin and leave to cool and set at room temperature overnight.

Turn the toffee out on to a chopping board and cut into 25 small squares using a large knife. The toffees look nice stored in a jar or wrapped in colourful paper.

Spicy 'Aztec' hot chocolate

Drinks, Spreads & Sauces

Spicy 'Aztec' hot chocolate

This is probably the oldest known hot chocolate recipe. The Aztecs used this spicy drink to give them power when going into battle. The combination of the dark chocolate and spices makes it a proper pick-me-up elixir – drink this and you will be ready to face any battle!

Serves 4
Preparation time: 5 minutes
Cooking time: 5 minutes

1 litre (1¾ pints) milk
100g (3½oz) dark chocolate, roughly chopped
2 tbsp light muscovado sugar
1 tsp ground cinnamon
1 tsp freshly grated nutmeg
1 tsp ground black pepper
100ml (3½fl oz) whipping cream
ground cinnamon and freshly grated nutmeg, for dusting

Put the milk into a heavy-based saucepan and bring to the boil. Reduce the heat, then add the chocolate, sugar and spices.

Using a small balloon whisk, whisk until the chocolate has completely melted. Simmer for 1 minute, then remove from the heat and whisk in the cream.

Pour into tall mugs and serve with a dusting of cinnamon and grated nutmeg. See previous page for the finished result.

1. Heat the milk and add the chocolate.

2. Add the sugar.

3. Then add the spices and whisk until the chocolate has melted.

4. Remove from the heat and whisk in the cream.

5. Pour into mugs.

6. Serve with a dusting of cinnamon and a grating of nutmeg.

Chocolate martini

There is something special about starting an evening with a martini cocktail. This chocolate version will surprise and amaze your guests, but watch out as it is a very smooth and easy-to-drink concoction…

Serves 1

Preparation time: 5 minutes, plus chilling

1 tbsp finely grated dark chocolate
50ml (2fl oz) whipping cream
1½ shots (60ml/2½fl oz) Irish cream liqueur
1½ shots (60ml/2½fl oz) crème de cacao
½ shot (20ml/1fl oz) vodka
ice cubes

First prepare your Manhattan glass. Using your fingertip, wet the rim of the glass with water. Scatter the grated chocolate on a small plate and turn the glass in the chocolate, making sure the rim is coated with chocolate. Chill in the refrigerator and reserve the remaining chocolate.

When ready to serve, lightly whip the cream until thickened slightly but still very sloppy. Put all the alcohol into a cocktail shaker with some ice cubes. Shake well, then pour it into the prepared chilled glass and add a twirl of the cream. Finish with a sprinkle of the reserved chocolate and serve immediately. Santé!

Chocolate and caramel cocktail

This is one of my favourite winter cocktails to serve to friends. It needs a bit of work but the good news is it can be prepared in advance. Be careful though, it is very moreish – drink in moderation.

Serves 3–4

Preparation time: 10 minutes, plus chilling

Cooking time: 5 minutes

15g (½oz) cocoa powder, plus 1 tsp
1 tsp sugar syrup
50g (2oz) golden caster sugar
4 tsp water
250ml (8fl oz) single cream
50ml (2fl oz) crème de cacao
50ml (2fl oz) orange liqueur
ice cubes

First prepare your glasses. Place the 1 teaspoon of cocoa powder and sugar syrup on separate saucers. Dip the rim of each glass into the syrup and then into the cocoa powder. Chill in the refrigerator.

Put the sugar and water into a heavy-based saucepan and heat gently until the sugar has dissolved, then increase the heat and cook until it forms a nice dark blond caramel. Add the cream and whisk in using a balloon whisk, scraping up the caramel from the bottom of the pan. Add the remaining cocoa powder and cook for a further 2 minutes, or until the mixture is smooth.

Pass through a sieve into a blender to remove any pieces of caramel, then add both liqueurs and blend for few minutes. Chill in the refrigerator.

When ready to serve, place some ice cubes in a cocktail shaker with the chilled cocktail and shake well. Pass it through a cocktail sieve, pour into the chilled glasses and serve immediately. Let's get the party started!

Double chocolate milkshake

This version of a classic chocolate milkshake reminds me of the first time I ate in a proper diner in the USA and had my first milkshake. A good shake should be creamy, thick and smooth, and leave you full – it's almost a dessert in a glass.

Serves 4

Preparation time: 5 minutes, plus chilling

Cooking time: 3 minutes

1 litre (1¾ pints) milk

100g (3½oz) dark chocolate, roughly chopped

4 large scoops of good-quality chocolate ice cream

2 tsp chocolate extract

2 tbsp malted milk powder

20 ice cubes

good-quality drinking chocolate powder, for dusting

Chill 4 tall serving glasses in the refrigerator.

Put the milk into a saucepan and heat to simmering point. Remove from the heat, add the chocolate and stir until completely melted. Leave to cool, then chill in the refrigerator for 10 minutes.

Pour the chocolate milk into a blender with the remaining ingredients. Blend at full speed until the mixture is light and frothy and there are no more ice crystals.

Pour into the chilled glasses, dust generously with drinking chocolate powder and serve immediately. Sit back and enjoy…

Chocolate and cola float

This is a reminder of those great soda parlours where as kids we were treated to fabulous Sunday outings. For me, the best treat was the cola float, as we never drank cola at home, so it was a double celebration! I wish soda parlours would make a comeback. In the meantime, try this updated recipe.

Serves 4

Preparation time: 10 minutes, plus chilling

250ml (8fl oz) double cream

1 litre (1¾ pints) cola (preferably the old-fashioned type)

2 tsp vanilla extract or paste

8 scoops of dark chocolate ice cream

100g (3½oz) maraschino cherries, plus a few extra to decorate

25g (1oz) dark chocolate, grated

Chill 4 tall sundae glasses in the refrigerator.

When ready to serve, lightly whip the cream until thickened slightly but still sloppy. Put to one side.

Put the cola, vanilla, ice cream and cherries into a large blender, in 2 batches if necessary, and use the pulse button to blend together.

Pour into the chilled glasses, spoon the cream on top and sprinkle over the grated chocolate. Decorate with a few maraschino cherries for a little touch of kitsch and serve immediately.

Tip

It is best to use the pulse button when blending the cola float, as it will fizz and froth a lot.

Conquistadors' hot cocoa

The conquistadors were responsible for introducing cocoa to Europe and this version of hot chocolate is also known as Spanish chocolate. I've added some Seville orange to it for an Iberian touch. This rich drink is best served with churros, the long Spanish doughnuts. A warning though – you can get hooked!

Serves 6–8
Preparation time: 5 minutes
Cooking time: 10 minutes

250ml (8fl oz) water
100g (3½oz) light muscovado sugar
2 tbsp cornflour
75g (3oz) cocoa powder
500ml (17fl oz) milk
grated zest of 1 orange
(Seville if in season)
1 tsp vanilla paste or extract
1 tsp pure orange extract (optional)

Put the water and sugar into a heavy-based saucepan and bring to the boil, stirring until the sugar has completely dissolved. Remove from the heat, sift the cornflour and cocoa powder together and whisk into the syrup using a small balloon whisk.

Return the pan to the heat and cook until the mixture forms a thick paste. Add the milk a little at a time, whisking continuously until smooth and glossy, then add the grated orange zest, vanilla and orange extract, if using. Simmer for 5 minutes, stirring continuously.

Serve piping hot in small warm coffee cups.

Tip

For a grown-up version, replace the orange extract with orange liqueur.

After-dinner mint hot chocolate

I know it is almost a tradition to serve after-dinner mint chocolates but why not serve a hot mint chocolate instead to impress your guests? It's one of my favourite dinner party tricks. I'm sure you and your friends will love it, too.

Serves 14–16
Preparation time: 10 minutes
Cooking time: 10 minutes

200g (7oz) light muscovado sugar
100g (3½oz) boiled mint sweets
500ml (17fl oz) water
125g (4oz) cocoa powder
2 tbsp cornflour
500ml (17fl oz) milk

Place the sugar and mint sweets in a food processor and blend to a fine powder. Put the water and sugar powder into a heavy-based saucepan and bring to the boil, stirring until the sugar powder has dissolved. Remove from the heat, sift the cocoa powder and cornflour together and whisk into the syrup using a small balloon whisk.

Return the pan to the heat and simmer until the mixture forms a smooth paste. Add the milk a little at a time, whisking until the mixture is smooth and glossy. Serve immediately in small heatproof shot glasses.

Proper Italian hot chocolate

When growing up, my family always went skiing during the festive seasons. We went to a small ski resort a few miles from Turin and our treat was this phenomenal thick hot chocolate called *cioccolata calda*. The legend goes: 'if your spoon doesn't stand up in your cup, it is not a proper one', but even I haven't managed to get mine to that legendary status!

Serves 6–8
Preparation time: 5 minutes
Cooking time: 15 minutes

1 litre (1¾ pints) milk
100g (3½oz) light muscovado sugar
100g (3½oz) cocoa powder
150ml (¼ pint) crème fraîche
2 tsp vanilla paste or extract

Put the milk and sugar into a heavy-based saucepan and heat gently until the sugar has dissolved. Remove from the heat and whisk in the cocoa powder and crème fraîche.

Return to a low heat and bring to a simmer, stirring. Simmer for about 10 minutes, or until thickened. Add the vanilla and whisk until frothy. Serve in small warm cups.

Mocha Brûlée

This extraordinary drink is a fantastic party piece that needs a little preparation but is worth all the effort.

Serves 4
Preparation time: 10 minutes
Cooking time: 5 minutes

800ml (1 pint 7fl oz) milk
4 shots of espresso coffee made with 200ml (7fl oz) just-boiled water
8 tbsp dark drinking chocolate powder
2 tsp vanilla paste or extract
4 tbsp demerara sugar

Put the milk into a saucepan and heat to just below boiling point.

Put the coffee into a heatproof bowl, add the drinking chocolate powder and stir until blended. Using a small balloon whisk, add 600ml (1 pint) of the hot milk a little at a time until the mixture is smooth. Stir in the vanilla, then pour into 4 warm flameproof coffee cups or small mugs.

Using an electric milk frother, froth the remaining hot milk. Spoon on top of the coffees and level it flat with a knife. Sprinkle the sugar over the froth in each glass and caramelize using a kitchen blowtorch. Serve immediately.

Tip

Skimmed milk froths more easily than semi-skimmed or full-fat milk.

Viennese chocolate

Vienna is known as the world capital of the coffee shop, where for hundreds of years they've served speciality coffee, pastries and other hot drinks. Viennese chocolate is certainly one of their most famous treats – pure indulgence in a glass.

Serves 4
Preparation time: 10 minutes
Cooking time: 10 minutes

200g (7oz) dark chocolate, roughly chopped
100ml (3½fl oz) whipping cream
25g (1oz) icing sugar
2 tsp vanilla sugar
1 litre (1¾ pints) milk
4 tbsp light muscovado sugar
cocoa powder and ground cinnamon, for dusting

Melt the chocolate in a heatproof bowl set over a saucepan of barely simmering water, making sure the surface of the water does not touch the bowl.

Meanwhile, whip the cream, icing sugar and vanilla sugar to stiff peaks and put to one side.

Put the milk and muscovado sugar into a saucepan and heat gently until the sugar has dissolved. Whisk in the melted chocolate a little at the time, then whisk over a low heat for at least 5 minutes, or until the mixture is smooth and glossy.

Pour the hot chocolate into 4 tall warm latte glasses. Scoop the cream nice and high on the tops, lightly dust with cocoa powder and cinnamon and serve immediately.

Hazelnut and chocolate spread

You can never beat homemade products and this spread is the absolute proof. It's a perfect breakfast treat spread generously on toasted brioche and it's also a great gift idea when presented in beautiful jars.

Makes 2 x 450g (1lb) jars

Preparation time: 5 minutes, plus cooling

Cooking time: 10 minutes

100g (3½oz) ground hazelnuts

150g (5oz) dark chocolate, roughly chopped

250g (8oz) unsalted butter

2 tsp vanilla paste or extract

400ml can condensed milk

2 tbsp hazelnut oil

Preheat the oven to 180°C (fan 160°C)/350°F/gas mark 4. Spread the ground hazelnuts on a baking sheet and roast for 3–4 minutes, or until a nice rich golden colour and the full aroma escapes from the oven. Leave to cool.

Melt the chocolate and one-quarter of the butter together in a small heatproof bowl set over a saucepan of barely simmering water, making sure the surface of the water does not touch the bowl. When melted, remove the saucepan from the heat but leave the bowl over the hot water. Stir in the roasted hazelnuts and the remaining ingredients until the mixture is smooth and glossy.

Pour into sterilized pots or jars (see Tip below), then leave to cool completely before sealing with the lids. Store in the refrigerator for up to 2 weeks. This is best removed from the refrigerator 1 hour before serving.

White chocolate spread

This rich, luxurious white chocolate spread is very easy to put together. It is the perfect accompaniment to toasted gingerbread or malt loaf.

Makes about 300ml (½ pint)

Preparation time: 5 minutes

Cooking time: 5 minutes

200g (7oz) white chocolate, roughly chopped

150ml (¼ pint) canned condensed milk

2 tsp vanilla paste

50ml (2fl oz) single cream

Melt all the ingredients together until smooth and glossy in a large heat-proof bowl set over a saucepan of barely simmering water, making sure the surface of the water does not touch the bowl.

Pour into small, sterilized pots or jars (see Tip below), then leave to cool completely before sealing with the lids. Store in the refrigerator for up to 2 weeks.

Tip

To sterilize jars, put clean, washed and dried jars into a cold oven with the lids off. Heat the oven to 180°C (fan 160°C)/350°F/gas mark 4 and leave for 20 minutes. Pour your chocolate spread into the jars while still warm from the oven.

Chocolate fondue

I know fondue is a bit retro, but a good chocolate fondue is a great alternative to a dessert or perfect for a party. You can be as creative as you want with the food to be dipped.

Serves 6

Preparation time: 15 minutes

Cooking time: 5 minutes

300g (10oz) dark chocolate, roughly chopped

2 tbsp milk

250ml (8fl oz) double cream

75g (3oz) unsalted butter, softened

1 tsp ground cinnamon

1 tsp vanilla paste or extract

2 tbsp dark rum

For dipping and coating

3 bananas, cut into chunky pieces

3 ripe pears, peeled, cored and cut into chunky pieces

juice of 1 lemon

12 large marshmallows

assortment of dried fruit, such as figs, dates and prunes

150g (5oz) chopped hazelnuts, roasted (see Tip on page 44)

150g (5oz) desiccated coconut

First prepare the dips. Toss the bananas and pears with the lemon juice to prevent browning. Arrange the prepared fruit, marshmallow and dried fruit on a large platter or in ramekins, together with the roasted nuts and coconut. Make a pile of metal or wooden kebab sticks on the side.

To make the fondue, place a fondue pan in a bain-marie. Alternatively, place a heatproof serving bowl over a saucepan of simmering water. Add the chocolate and milk and melt together, then whisk in the cream. Keep warm, then just before serving stir in the butter, cinnamon, vanilla and rum.

Take the warm fondue to the table hot and encourage people to help themselves. Use the kebab sticks to dip the fruits and marshmallows into the hot chocolate, then roll into the nuts or coconut. A fun way to end a dinner party!

Four ultimate chocolate sauces

Chocolate sauces are a perfect accompaniment to desserts, crêpes, waffles and ice cream. Here I've penned four of my favourite ones.

Dark chocolate sauce

Makes 500ml (17fl oz)
Preparation time: 5 minutes
Cooking time: 2 minutes

125ml (4fl oz) milk
125ml (4fl oz) single cream
50g (2oz) golden caster sugar
200g (7oz) dark chocolate, chopped
50g (2oz) unsalted butter, softened

Put the milk, cream and sugar into a saucepan and heat gently until the sugar has dissolved. Remove from the heat and add the chocolate, stirring until melted. Stir in the butter. Serve warm on ice cream or over profiteroles, or chill, then serve with cake or crêpes.

Irish cream chocolate sauce

Make the dark chocolate sauce as above, stirring in 3 tbsp Irish cream liqueur after adding the butter.

Zesty white chocolate sauce

Makes about 300ml (½ pint)
Preparation time: 5 minutes
Cooking time: 2 minutes

150ml (¼ pint) single cream

4 tbsp milk

200g (7oz) white chocolate, chopped

grated zest of 1 lemon

1 tbsp extra virgin olive oil

Put the cream and milk into a saucepan and bring to the boil. Remove from the heat and stir in the chocolate until melted and smooth, then stir in the lemon zest and olive oil. This superb combination is perfect for fruity, summery desserts.

Milk chocolate and hazelnut sauce

Makes about 300ml (½ pint)
Preparation time: 5 minutes
Cooking time: 5 minutes

200g (7oz) milk chocolate, roughly chopped

75ml (3fl oz) single cream

1 tsp vanilla extract

2 tsp clear honey

25g (1oz) ground hazelnuts, roasted (see Tip on page 44)

Melt the chocolate in a heatproof bowl set over a saucepan of barely simmering water, making sure the surface of the water does not touch the bowl. Stir in the cream, vanilla and honey until smooth and glossy, then stir in the ground hazelnuts. Serve warm over ice cream, pancakes or fruit.

Chocolate glaze

This is a perfect, delicious recipe to spread over cakes or treats like brownies. The easy glaze is rich, smooth and glossy, so it also works very well as a paint for those of you ready to express your artistic flair on fruit, plates or body parts!

Makes 150ml (¼ pint)
Preparation time: 2 minutes
Cooking time: 3 minutes

125g (4oz) dark chocolate, roughly chopped
50g (2oz) unsalted butter
1 tbsp golden syrup
1 tsp vanilla extract or paste

Melt the chocolate, butter and golden syrup together in a heatproof bowl set over a saucepan of barely simmering water, making sure the surface of the water does not touch the bowl. Stir occasionally, until smooth and glossy, then add the vanilla.

Using a palette knife, spread the glaze over cakes or brownies.

Tip

If you are feeling artistic, decorate fruit and plates (or body parts!) with the chocolate glaze using a fine clean paintbrush.

Index

All recipes use dark chocolate except those listed as milk or white chocolate

Author acknowledgements

Author's acknowledgements

This book wouldn't have happened without the continuous support of Denise Bates and her team at Mitchell Beazley. A big thank you to Alison Starling for bringing the 'A' team together and making sure than the long process to create this book went smoothly with a fabulous end result. All the way through the book my recipes are showcased and styled in a beautiful way to still look accessible with a naughty indulgent side! As with the last 3 books, Juliette and Sybella have done a fantastic job with both the design and deciphering my bad English. The combination of their talents, as well as the gorgeous photography from the talented Kate Whitaker and styling by Liz Belton, make this book really stand out.

This is my first book featuring a single, main ingredient and I must thank both Wendy Lee, my food economist, for testing all the recipes, and to Rachel Wood for helping me recreate them for the photo shoot … sorry girls, if I've put you off chocolate for a while! I am sure your taste for it will be back soon. As usual, we had a great time working together and much laughter, we all deserved that homemade fried chicken with vintage champagne we all shared together on the last day.

Time to thank, too, the team I call Team Eric: Annie, my agent, Jean my publicist and my team at Cake Boy for their continuous support and help. Many thanks to Fiona at Mitchell Beazley and Liz at Hachette USA for their belief and hard work to promote this gorgeous book, of which I am very proud.

A bientot pour le prochain livre!

Eric x